Rembrandt

Rembrandt

Rembrandt

Michael Kitson

Phaidon • Oxford

Phaidon Press Limited, Littlegate House, St Ebbe's Street, Oxford OX1 1SQ

First published 1969
This edition, revised and enlarged, first published 1982
© Phaidon Press 1982

British Library Cataloguing in Publication Data

Kitson, Michael
 Rembrandt. —3rd ed. rev. and enl. — (Phaidon colour library
 1. Rembrandt
 I. Title   II. Rembrandt
 759.9492   ND653.R4

 ISBN 0–7148–2228–0
 ISBN 0–7148–2241–8 Pbk

Typeset, printed and bound in Singapore under co-ordination by Graphic Consultants International Private Limited

The Publishers have endeavoured to credit all known persons holding copyright or reproduction rights for the illustrations in this book. Particular acknowledgement is made for the following: Fig. 30 – Museum 'Het Rembrandthuis', Amsterdam; Plates 24 and 27 (Gemäldegalerie) and Plate 5, Figs. 13 and 25 (Kupferstichkabinett), Staatliche Museen Preussischer Kulturbesitz, West Berlin; Plate 12 — The Trustees of the Chatsworth House Trust Ltd.; Fig. 27 — The Collection of the Art Institute of Chicago; Figures 1, 2, 7, 19, 22, 26, 28, 29, 34 and 45 — Reproduced by Courtesy of the Trustees of the British Museum, London; Plate 21 — By permission of the Governors of the Dulwich Picture Gallery, London; Plates 11, 20, 29, 30, 40 and Figs. 10, 12, 20 and 38 — Reproduced by courtesy of the Trustees, The National Gallery, London; Plate 2 — Reproduced by permission of the National Gallery of Victoria, Melbourne; Fig. 15 — Bayerische Staatsgemaldesammlung, Alte Pinakothek, Munich; Plate 34 — Copyright The Frick Collection, New York; Figs. 24 and 36 — Fondation Custodia (Collection F. Lugt), Institut Néerlandais, Paris; Figs. 31 and 32 – Musée du Louvre, Paris; Plate 15 — The Norton Simon Foundation at Pasadena; Figs. 6, 17 and 42 — Graphische Sammlung Albertina, Vienna; Plates 37 and 46 and Fig. 44 — The National Gallery of Art, Washington D.C., Widener Collection.

Rembrandt

When we stand in the Rembrandt room of a major picture gallery, what visual impressions do we receive there and how do they differ from the impressions we receive from the works of other artists in the gallery?

To begin with, we notice dark backgrounds broken by irregular patches of light. There is more dark than light, and the light does not often extend as far as the frame. Instead, it lies in or near the centre, where it balances the dark and holds most of our attention. Usually there are both black and white in the picture, the black occurring in a robe or hat, the white in a collar, cuffs or else in a headcloth or shirtfront. The frames are also sometimes black. Black and white represent colours — the only unmodified colours in the picture — but they also register as extremes of light and dark tones.

Otherwise the paintings are rich in colour but it is not pure or evenly applied colour; nor is the composition divided into fields of different colours as in Renaissance or modern painting. Even in Rembrandt's early works the colours are broken and changing, like a brocade woven with gold or silver threads or like the glowing embers of a fire. In the highlights and deepest shadows the colours almost disappear. In the middle tones they deepen and become more intense in one of two directions: either towards red (vermilion or madder lake) or towards greenish-gold. It is typical of Rembrandt that he uses these colours as alternatives, not together, so that red and green seldom appear in combination. Except in some of his earliest works he generally avoids colour contrasts and complementaries and prefers colours close to each other in the spectrum. Brown, orange or yellow are mixed with or appear beside red; yellow or dull green accompany and merge into greenish-gold. Grey is also used with his two main colours.

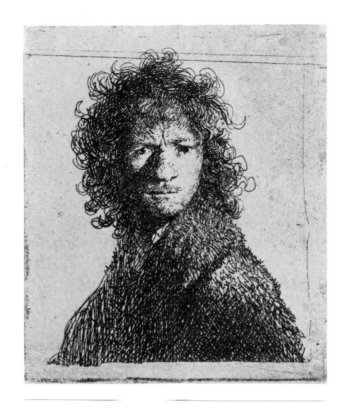

Fig. 1
Self-Portrait

ETCHING, 7.2 × 6.1 CM. SIGNED WITH MONOGRAM AND DATED, 1630.
LONDON, BRITISH MUSEUM

Blues, violets, pinks and bright greens, however, occur only in pale tints and in subordinate positions. The early paintings are generally cool in colour, the mature and late ones warm, with red predominating. Like the strongest lights, the strongest colours are confined to only a comparatively small part of the picture. The effect is of a surge of colour coming from within the form rather than of colour decorating the surface, defining the form's shape.

The backgrounds are also of no single colour but are made up of dull browns, greens and

5

greys, usually blended together but in the late works sometimes laid on side by side. Unlike the backgrounds of some Italian baroque painters, Rembrandt's are never flat or opaque but are filled with atmosphere and penetrated by reflected light. (Only uncleaned paintings by Rembrandt give an impression of solid dark brown in the shadows.) These subdued background colours register as tones. Tone, or rather *chiaroscuro* (light and shade), is the basis of Rembrandt's art. Colour, however important and beautiful, is contingent. It may be quite strong or very restrained; some paintings are almost monochromatic, and a few are executed in *grisaille* (brownish-grey). But whatever its strength, colour is an adjunct. The scheme of the composition is established by the *chiaroscuro*. Colour is applied in some parts, where it attracts the eye and heightens the emotional tension, but not in others. Only in certain late works does colour become a semi-independent medium, and even predominate (Plate 38). Elsewhere it is integrated with the *chiaroscuro*. *Chiaroscuro* is the principal means both of 'keeping together the overall harmony' (as Rembrandt's earliest biographer, Sandrart, put it) and of creating a poetic mood; it is also a source of aesthetic pleasure and of luminous and striking effects in its own right. Rembrandt's mastery of *chiaroscuro*, in all its degrees from the darkest darks to the strongest lights, has been acknowledged ever since his own time.

In composition, Rembrandt's paintings are essentially simple and stable and are built up from the edges towards the centre. Secondary lights, colours and forms are subordinated to primary ones. Rembrandt does not divide up the design into distinct self-contained units or distribute the interest among different areas of the picture. Visually the design obeys a principle of hierarchy. Except in his earliest works there is no sense of overcrowding or strain. Movement continues to be represented somewhat later (during his 'baroque' period) but after a while it too largely disappears. At all stages of his development his figures possess great authority and presence. They are set against a background which is vague and neutral enough not to compete with them yet which is everywhere visually interesting. Thus the background forms part of the design; it is not a mere backcloth. It also serves to relax the tension which exists at and near the centre and to effect a smooth transition from the imagined world of the main action or figure to the real world of the spectator.

Elegance, *contrapposto*, the harmony and balance of parts — those foundations on which the beautiful rests in Renaissance painting — are conspicuous by their absence. Except in Rembrandt's most baroque paintings there are no swinging lines and few three-dimensional curves or forms leading the eye into depth. He sometimes borrows from, but is never dependent upon, conventional formulas of the ideal and the beautiful. He uses flat, often rather fastidious and simple shapes lying parallel to the picture surface, especially in his late period, but not graceful, sweeping contours or variations of the S-curve common to mannerist, baroque and rococo painters. When he does introduce a curving or flowing line he interrupts its rhythm with some irregular twist or sudden change in pace. Generally speaking, flowing lines are weak in Rembrandt; jagged or straight lines are energetic. In some of his late works he builds up a pattern of rectangles and triangles, and occasionally a large circle or disc appears in the background (Plate 41). After the early years of his career, in keeping with his unwillingness to use a stressed contour, he tends to avoid figures and faces in profile. He prefers to contain the most interesting visual effects *within* the contour of the form, as in the *Jewish Bride* (Plate 47), in which the man's right hand and both the woman's form a pattern of hands in the centre of the composition.

To an unusual degree Rembrandt's art — not only in his portraits but also in his subject pictures — is dominated by faces; few of them are handsome and many of the most remarkable are old. Their watchful eyes are indistinct and often in shadow except for a line of light along the lids. His faces are always expressive and habitually tense. An urge to communicate thought, feeling and experience is imprinted on them. Although partly shadowed, they are seen in close-up, as if the artist were peering at them and they were returning his gaze. From the works of few other artists do we get such a sense of watching and of being watched. It is not an accident that about two-thirds of Rembrandt's paintings are portraits (including some thirty of himself). Most of the rest in our hypothetical Rembrandt room will be scenes or figures from the Bible. In addition, there will probably be a mythological scene, a landscape and perhaps a *genre* scene or still-life. The paintings are likely to vary greatly in size and to range from the very small to the very large.

Permeating all Rembrandt's works of whatever category and size is an air of solemnity and mystery. He is not a frivolous or merely sensuous artist, nor does he delight in beauty of colour or brushwork for their own sake. When colour and brushwork are beautiful, as they often are, they are so for expressive rather than decorative reasons. Moreover, the solemn and the mysterious are attributes of Rembrandt's style, not merely of his attitude to the subject-matter. To veil forms, textures and colours, leaving something for the imagination to fill in, is central to his method. A tone, a background, suggests more than it states; the eye can only trace out its implications so far. The world of Rembrandt's paintings is certainly as imaginary as that of any classicizing painter working in an ideal style: he seldom takes us into the open air or reconstructs a real interior. Yet, unlike the world of most imaginative painters, his is not raised above nature; it appears to us rather as an intensified version of nature's essential reality. Rembrandt reverses the normal procedure of idealizing artists. Whereas they transform the essence of things and leave a reminder of nature in the details, he preserves reality in the essence and clothes its outward forms with a mysterious beauty and suggestiveness.

It is useful to begin thus by recalling some of the aesthetic characteristics of Rembrandt's paintings, because for over a hundred years the praise of Rembrandt was often less aesthetic than moral — though there has been some reaction against this recently. Until about a decade ago his work was treated as the product not so much of a visual artist as of an inspired Protestant saint. The emphasis fell on his possession of qualities of character: dedication, humanity, compassion, spiritual and psychological insight, courage to ignore fashion and to refuse to flatter patrons, above all, unswerving devotion to 'the truth' — the truth about himself, his sitters and the events and characters of the Bible. These qualities were immediately attractive. Integrity and independence of spirit in artists were perceived to be the highest good. Nor is it intrinsically an error to see Rembrandt in this light, although it is possible to exaggerate the extent to which he possessed some of the virtues attributed to him. Nevertheless, it is important to be aware of what had happened. That is to say, we should realize that much of the post-Romantic tendency of Rembrandt appreciation was due to developments in art criticism since his time and that what was seen in his work may not have been either apparent to his contemporaries or present in the consciousness of Rembrandt himself. For some reason this phenomenon is particularly acute where Rembrandt is concerned. It may be so partly because contemporary information about his *art* is very hard to obtain, whereas his personality — and hence by unconscious inference his mind — is deceptively accessible, through documents relating to his life, through his self-portraits, through his portraits of his family, and so on. But whatever the reason, the result was to divert attention from Rembrandt the artist to Rembrandt the man. Thus there emerged a sentimental cult of Rembrandt, which was not by any means confined to popular or old-fashioned literature; this cult presented us with Rembrandt the home-lover, the paragon of virtue and the sage.

It is not easy to tell how far the post-Romantic Rembrandt, even without the sentimental distortions, was the invention, and how far the discovery, of later critics. It would be as foolish to ignore the insights of the past hundred and fifty years as it would be to accept them without question. What is certain is that they were made possible by a radical shift in the methods of criticism which began in the Romantic period. The practice of previous critics had been to assess the qualities of a work of art by examining the work itself; the tendency now was to look beyond the work and to seek for the key to its qualities in the artist's mind. The significance of this development for the understanding of Rembrandt is so great that it is worth discussing it a little further.

Until the Romantics, works of art had been assessed with reference to more or less objective standards. They were judged by whether they were beautiful or ugly, true or false to nature, and whether or not they were executed in accordance with certain rules. They were examined piecemeal, under the headings of drawing, colour, composition, etc. With the coming of Romanticism, standards became at once more comprehensive and more subjective. Sincerity was used as a criterion of artistic judgement for the first time and new kinds of truth were brought into the argument. Was the artist true to his own inner vision and experience (that is, was he sincere)? Did he, as Goethe once expressed it, 'love what he painted and paint only what he loved'? Was he true not just to the letter but to the spirit of his subject-matter? In this way the critical interest was shifted from the work of art to the artist's total vision.

As a result of these developments, what had previously been regarded as faults or at best limitations in Rembrandt came to be considered merits. His 'low' subjects and interest in and association with the poor, the old and the Jews, which had been condemned as undignified, now marked him out as the champion of the downtrodden and the oppressed; hence the concept of Rembrandt's compassion emerged. His broad brushwork and disregard of the rules of proportion and anatomy, which had been thought ignorant and eccentric, were now interpreted as a refusal to sacrifice his convictions for the sake of easy fame; hence arose the idea of Rembrandt's integrity. His common, naturalistic style, once thought fit only for comic and vulgar subjects, was now felt to be better suited to scenes from the Bible than the ideal style of the Italians, since those scenes took place in humble surroundings and were enacted by humble people; hence came the discovery of Rembrandt's spiritual insight and regard for truth.

The question of the special appropriateness of Rembrandt's style for religious subject-matter is of particular interest, as it has played so large a part in modern criticism and in forming the popular image of Rembrandt even today. Probably the first to discuss this point was Goethe, in the essay from which the phrase quoted earlier was taken (*Nach Falkonet und über Falkonet*, 1776). This essay already contains, in essence, everything that has been said on the subject since, and says it with a moderation not always found in later writings. Rembrandt is seen as having created a new form of religious art, as valid in its way as Raphael's was in another way. Indeed, his style had the advantage over Italian Renaissance painting in being truer than the latter to the spirit of the Bible, and hence of being fresher and more capable of communicating the Christian message with an appropriate directness and force.

'When Rembrandt represents his Madonna and Child as a Dutch peasant woman, it is easy for every refined gentleman to see that this is historically inaccurate, since we are told that Christ was born in Bethlehem of Judaea. The Italians did it better! he says. And how, please? — did Raphael paint anything other, anything more, than a loving mother with her first-born and only son? and what else could have been made of the subject? Has not mother-love in its joys and sorrows been a fruitful subject for poets and painters in all ages? But all the Bible stories have been

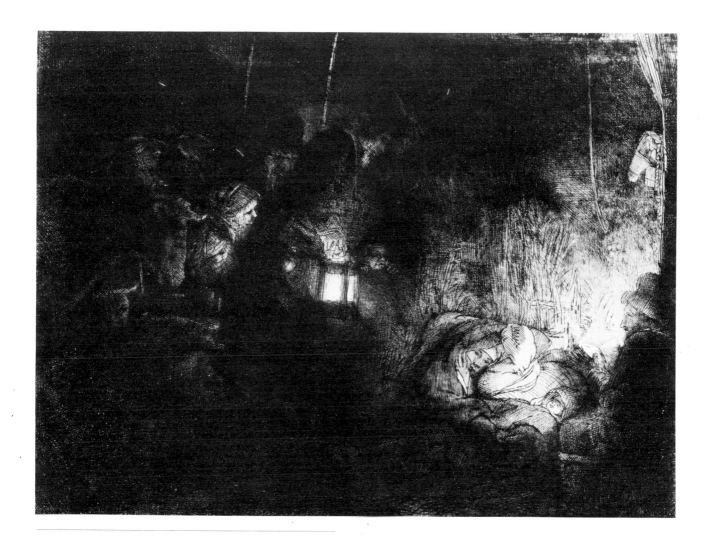

Fig. 2
The Adoration of the Shepherds

ETCHING, 14.9 × 19.6 CM C.1656. LONDON, BRITISH MUSEUM

deprived of their simplicity and truth by cold grandeur and stiff ecclesiastical propriety, and have thus been withdrawn from sympathetic hearts in order to dazzle the gaping eyes of the stupid. Does not Mary sit between the scrolls of every altar-frame, before the shepherds, as if she were displaying her Child for money, or as if she had rested for four weeks after her confinement so as to prepare with the vanity of a lady for the honour of this visit? Now that's decent! that's proper! that doesn't trespass against history!

How does Rembrandt treat this subject ⌊the late etching of *The Adoration of the Shepherds*, Fig. 2]? He places us in a dark stable; necessity has driven the mother, the Child at her breast, to share a bed with the cattle. They are both wrapped to the neck in straw and rags, and everything is dark outside the glow from a small lamp which shines on the father, who sits there with a small book and appears to read Mary a prayer. At this moment the shepherds enter. The foremost of them, who advances with a stable-lantern, peers, taking off his cap, into the straw. Was it possible more clearly to express the question: Is this the new-born King of the Jews?'

The key to this passage lies in the change of tone at the beginning of the second paragraph. No one before had described a composition by Rembrandt so literally and so sympathetically or had so well caught its spirit of simple humility. Here for the first time Rembrandt is presented as the painter of and for the human heart.

As has already been said, these considerations

9

are not irrelevant or invalid. There is no doubt that Rembrandt did introduce a new kind of religious art, based on a literal rather than symbolic interpretation of the Bible. What is more, whoever looks at his work, and not only at his religious paintings but also at his portraits and even landscapes, cannot help seeing it as a moral as well as an aesthetic achievement. But while this is true, it is a method of approach to Rembrandt which lies in the background of this essay, whose purpose is, rather, to return to an older tradition of criticism and to discuss his paintings as works of art. Its theme is Rembrandt the artist. We see a painting of *The Holy Family with Angels* (Plate 22). It strikes us as simultaneously domestic and sacred, lively and serene, intimate and deeply moving. How were the tones, colours and brushmarks disposed to produce these results? This is the type of question that will chiefly concern us.

Rembrandt as an Artist

Although little information relating to Rembrandt's art (as distinct from his life) has come down to us, such as it is it is not negligible and is worth briefly recalling. It appears chiefly in the following sources: the three earliest biographies of the artist, by Sandrart (1675), Baldinucci (1686) and Houbraken (1718); a treatise on painting by one of his pupils, Samuel van Hoogstraten (1678); the journal of Constantyn Huygens (who visited Rembrandt and his colleague Lievens in Leyden in or about 1629); a small group of letters to Huygens from Rembrandt; the inventory of his collection of works of art (both by himself and by and after other artists), weapons and curios, drawn up at his bankruptcy in 1656; and, last but not least, his own work. By this is meant, not his work in its entirety, but those aspects of it, particularly drawings and etchings, which reveal through their subject-matter the personal background to his activity as a painter. This is not the place to examine these sources in detail, as the information contained in them is often indirect and would require lengthy interpretation, but some general points emerge which are worth discussing in relation to Rembrandt's practice as an artist.

Not unnaturally, the three early biographers of Rembrandt judged him by the standards of their own time. They were by no means insensitive to his qualities and they found him to be an artist of extraordinary power. They praised his colour and *chiaroscuro* and Houbraken particularly stressed the variety and vividness of the poses of his figures and their facial expressions and gestures. On the other hand, they criticized him for being weak in drawing and for neglecting the classical rules of proportion and anatomy, especially in his treatment of the nude. His paintings were believed to be unfinished owing to their broad brushwork and heavy impasto, and he was scarcely mentioned as a painter of religious subjects; rather, he was regarded (at least by Sandrart) as a *genre* painter who mostly chose subjects to please himself from the everyday life around him.

In regarding Rembrandt in this way the biographers were applying the standards of ideal art. Nowadays it is generally agreed that where Rembrandt is concerned these standards are largely irrelevant. However, this does not mean that his attitude to them was one of simple rejection, still less that he was unaware of them. Even though he never visited Italy he had ample opportunity to study Italian paintings, drawings and engravings in collections and at auction sales in Amsterdam (as he told Huygens); he could follow the example of those of his predecessors, including his teacher Lastman, who had been to Italy; and he could read, in Dutch, Van Mander's long 'Didactic Poem' on painting, published in Haarlem in 1604 together with his *Lives of the Artists*, in which the theory of ideal art was fully expounded. Up to a point, in fact, this theory – sometimes called the 'classical-idealist' theory of art because of its roots in classical antiquity – must have furnished the aesthetic assumptions on which his own art was based, if only because there was no other articulated body of theory available, not merely in Dutch but in any European language. Two of its principles in particular apply: the doctrine of the superiority of history painting over all other genres, and the importance of illustrating a subject and depicting the emotions appropriate to it by means of gestures and facial expressions. As to the first, it should be remembered that, despite the biographers, Rembrandt was a 'history painter' hardly less than Raphael or Rubens, although of a very different kind. His works, like theirs, were scenes from sacred history and (less often) classical history and mythology — imaginative in conception, moral in content and serious in mood. So anxious was he from the first to succeed in this branch of art that he never painted a commissioned portrait in his Leyden years. It is further evident that, although there was no demand in Holland for paintings to decorate churches, Rembrandt's religious pictures, not to mention his etchings, often found buyers among private collectors.

Rembrandt's interest in the illustration of the subject and the rendering of emotion is even more significant. Overtly and dramatically in his early period, more subtly in his middle and later years, Rembrandt was one of the great storytellers of art. This did not mean only that he chose a promising situation or narrative and depicted it clearly, but also that he extracted the utmost

emotional significance from it. His earliest self-portraits (see Fig. 1) are exercises in expression, and in his subject pictures throughout his career he showed feelings — in faces and in the way people stood or sat and used their hands — with a vividness and variety unsurpassed in painting. Rembrandt's skill in this art was noticed early in his career by Huygens as well as some time after his death by Houbraken. It was also the subject of the one revealing comment on art in Rembrandt's own letters, which are otherwise predominantly about money. Describing to Huygens (12 January 1639) the *Entombment* (Fig. 15) and the *Resurrection of Christ*, which he had just completed for Prince Frederick-Henry, Rembrandt states that in them he had represented 'the greatest and most natural movement' (*die meeste ende die naetureelste beweechgelickheyt*). There is some doubt whether the last word in this phrase should be translated as movement or emotion; in fact it probably implies both (there is a similar double meaning in the English word 'moving') since mobility of poses, faces and gestures was the normal means by which emotion was expressed. In this way the phrase would be applicable not only to the *Resurrection*, in which there is a great deal of violent physical movement, but also to the outwardly calmer, though equally emotional, *Entombment*. It is an interesting coincidence that, in the same year, Poussin was writing in the same sense (but at much greater length) to his patron, Chantelou, about the depiction of emotions in *The Gathering of Manna*.

However, Rembrandt's awareness of the theory of ideal art and his acceptance of two of its most widely known principles did not mean that he was deeply interested in this theory or that he adhered to it uncritically. Although he probably had a number of aesthetic maxims which he was fond of repeating to his pupils (who in turn passed them on in garbled form to the authors of the early sources), it is unlikely that he had any fully-fledged artistic theory. And in some important respects he positively rejected the principles of ideal art. According to both Sandrart and Hoogstraten, he laid particular stress on the imitation of nature, even going so far as to state that 'the artist should be guided by nature and by no other rules'. This, if true, would have been a direct contradiction of classical principles, according to which artists should use the rules and the example of the art of the past as a means of 'correcting' nature. Furthermore, Rembrandt was not concerned with the doctrine of decorum, or the matching of style with subject-matter. Nor was he committed to following the Antique, or Raphael, or the classical ideal of beauty, although he made use of all three on occasions and although his collection contained many examples of classical sculpture, either in the original or in casts, and several complete sets of engravings after Raphael. Whenever he referred to these sources in his work or painted a nude or a figure in some classical attitude, he produced a free adaptation. Even if only slightly, he undermined the system of ideal art at the point where it was most vulnerable: in its rule of internal consistency. He would interrupt the flow of a form with a quirk of realism, thicken (say) the proportions of the legs in relation to the rest of the body, or make the weight of the figure greater than its form would lead one to expect. And he did all this, unlike his Flemish and Dutch predecessors who had only half understood the classical rules, without sacrificing the organic unity of the figure or of the painting as a whole.

In his early period one can see Rembrandt almost 'attacking' the Antique. He represents the youthful Ganymede abducted by the eagle as a yelling, urinating baby. Two or three years earlier he produced a black chalk drawing of a Rubensian *Diana*, in which he made the arms and legs thinner, the flesh flabbier and the face more innocent than Rubens would have done. He subsequently used this drawing as the basis of an etching, removing the bow and quiver of Diana, adding still more creases to the flesh and turning the result into a harshly realistic study of a naked young woman. The object of these exercises was surely to strike a blow against art and on behalf of nature, and hence on behalf of artistic freedom. But Rembrandt's assault on the classical rules of art was also a means of understanding them. Out of that understanding grew the *Danaë* in Leningrad (Fig. 3), Rembrandt's nearest approach to a traditional classical nude. But by the standards of Titian or Raphael even this is imperfect; the head and hands are too large, the facial expression is too eager and one breast is pressed awkwardly out of shape by its position against the left hand. After these early experiments Rembrandt's confrontation with classicism was never again so direct or so highly charged; he never came so close either to accepting it, as in the *Danaë*, or to rejecting it completely, as in the *Ganymede*. In his later work, his attitude towards it is subtle, unexpected and oblique.

Freedom is the keynote of Rembrandt's relationship not only to the classical ideal but to other styles and traditions of art as well. What has just been said about his attitude to the Antique and the theory of ideal art could also be applied to his artistic relationships with Dürer, Leonardo and Titian (who is perhaps the artist with whom his affinity is closest, although the resemblances between his late work and that of the Venetian may be due to coincidence). Moving nearer to Rembrandt's own country and time, there are similar analogies to be found with the work of Elsheimer, Rubens and Seghers. Rembrandt's use of all these, and other, sources was selective and flexible. We have seen one example of the way in which his flexibility showed itself: his treatment of the classical nude. But his freedom of approach had many more consequences than this. He could paint 'high' subject-matter in a 'low' style (thus breaking the classical rule of decorum). He could combine the beautiful and the ugly, the majestic and the ordinary and, most important of all, the supernatural and the real. While accepting the obligation enjoined by classical art-theory to re-

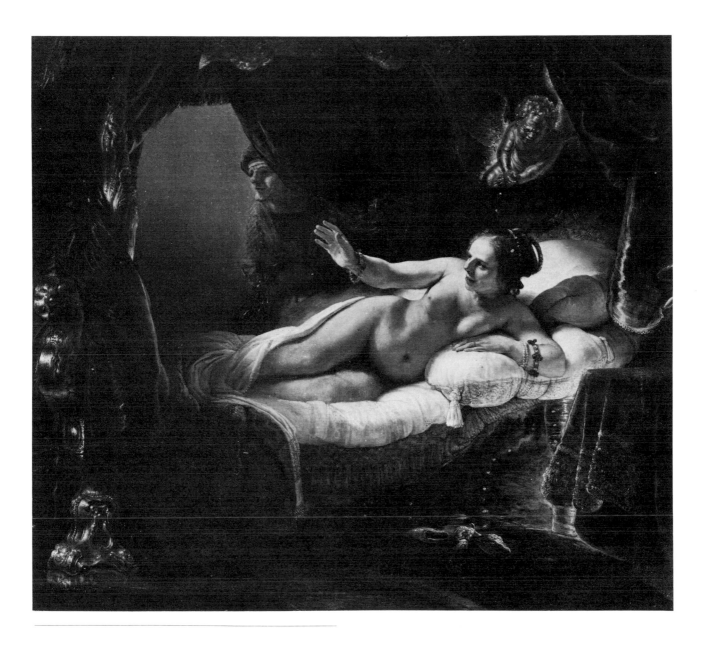

Fig. 3
Danaë

CANVAS, 185 × 203 CM. SIGNED 'REMBRANDT F. 16(3)6'. LENINGRAD,
THE HERMITAGE

present emotion in his figures, he succeeded in evolving a new, naturalistic method of doing it. It was a method quite different from that originally devised by Italian Renaissance artists, which elsewhere in Europe during his lifetime was hardening into a formula. As will be seen later, Rembrandt's method was in effect no method, but an apparently direct depiction of the feelings experienced by a figure, which he achieved as much by relying on the surrounding context and by means of the *chiaroscuro* and brushwork as by using movements of the facial muscles or gestures with the hands.

Furthermore, Rembrandt (though in this he was like several other Dutch artists) ignored the convention, which was inherent in the theory of ideal art, according to which the different categories of painting should be kept distinct from one another. With him, religious subjects may be treated like *genre* scenes (see Plate 1); portraits may merge in one direction into paintings of saints or mythological characters (Plate 9), in another direction into studies of anonymous models (Plate 33). However, there was one distinction which Rembrandt did maintain: that between subjects appropriate to paintings and those he regarded as suitable only for drawings (his etchings characteristically occupy a middle position between the two). Whereas his drawings include many *genre* scenes (Fig. 24), *genre* figures (Fig. 21) and landscapes studied from nature (Figs. 6 and 27), his paintings on the whole do not. As a painter, Rembrandt was concerned with man as a human and spiritual being, and to have shown, in his paintings, man in the passing context of his day-to-day environment and activities, as he did in his drawings, would have detracted from that concern. Thus, after a few early experiments, he abandoned the painting of *genre* scenes and transferred the element of *genre* into the representation of domestic scenes from the Old and New Testament. Nor was this merely a nominal transposition, for the whole character of the subject is subtly altered, not just its outward details. In these paintings, a common Dutch pictorial form — the *genre* scene — and a deeply rooted social preoccupation — the home — are given a heightened poetic significance by their treatment as a religious subject.

It would be possible to see this characteristic in Rembrandt as a kind of idealism, and hence as the expression of an attitude similar to that which underlay the theory of ideal art. Nor would this be wrong, provided we interpret his expression of that attitude as, typically, a very personal one and regard his preoccupation with man's spiritual state more as a spontaneous development in him than as the product of any obvious outside influence. Moreover, it is reflected not only in his assimilation of everyday subject-matter to religious art, but also in his treatment of the painted single figure which was neither a portrait nor a character from the Bible or classical mythology. It is customary in catalogues and convenient for purposes of discussion to classify these figures as '*genre* studies'. But this is precisely what they are not, for they lack that distinguishing feature of *genre*, namely the element of anecdote and the hint, however slight, of activity. Rembrandt's single figures do nothing but think. To call such figures as the *Young Girl Leaning on a Window-Sill* (Plate 21) or the *Two Negroes* (Plate 44) *genre* studies is to diminish their significance.

There is also something else. Just as these paintings have a more profound *content* than other Dutch paintings of single figures, so they have a less explicit *subject*. It is impossible to attach an allegorical label to them, like one of the Five Senses or *Vanitas*, any more than they can be called figures drinking, playing music, reading a letter or trying on a pearl necklace, for they do none of these things. Their lack of subject in the ordinary meaning of the term may be reflected in Sandrart's report that Rembrandt painted subjects 'that are ordinary and without special significance, subjects that pleased him and were picturesque (*schilderachtig*), as the people of the Netherlands say.' As a critical comment this is misleading, as it implies that Rembrandt was motivated by that idle curiosity which produces *genre*, yet the absence of an identifiable subject in these paintings was sufficiently remarkable for Sandrart to think it worth recording. It may even be the case that some of Rembrandt's paintings in which the figure is dressed in an exotic costume may belong to this category. These figures are usually interpreted nowadays as characters from the Bible, but Rembrandt may not have intended anything so specific, at least when he conceived the figure, although he may have attached a name to it afterwards. Perhaps even the famous and mysterious

Polish Rider (Plate 34), over which modern scholars have speculated endlessly in an attempt to find a title that would fit it, is a painting of this type. Be that as it may, Rembrandt's develop- ment of the single-figure study with no explicit subject as a serious independent art form was not the least of his contributions to the future of European painting.

The Subject Pictures

The term 'subject pictures' here covers paint- ings, whether of religious or mythological themes, in which a situation or story is repre- sented. In this section we shall be concerned with the way Rembrandt developed his style and technique in these pictures, which of their na- ture usually contain two or more figures. The problems of the single figure, which have already been touched on, will be discussed further in the next section, under portraits.

Rembrandt's earliest subject pictures (Plates 1 and 2) are small, crowded and highly finished. They are designed to be examined minutely at close range. In style and often in subject they depend on his teacher, Lastman (Fig. 4); they also contain echoes, transmitted through Last- man, of the intense, exotic art of Elsheimer. Their subjects tend to be taken from some minor episode in the Bible or from ancient history, which lent itself to the narrative treatment fami- liar to contemporary Dutch artists. As paintings they are primitive and awkward. Their forms are lumpy, their poses complicated, and each figure seems to have been studied on its own, to be joined to the others afterwards. Hands gesti- culate, eyes are beady and mouths drawn down. The flesh even of quite young figures appears to be shrivelled up like a wizened apple. There is often a figure in the foreground in shadow seen from the back. It is evident that, like many young artists, Rembrandt was keeping a close eye on the art around him and, knowing he would be judged by its standards, trying to outdo it. We

can sense him hoping to win through by a display of skill. He would expect each figure to be ad- mired in turn. At the same time, he was bolder than Lastman, who seems by comparison fright- ened of disobeying the classical rules. He avoids Lastman's generalized forms and draperies; from the start Rembrandt is concerned with the particular. An individual vein of appealing senti- ment informs the *Anna and Tobit* (Plate 1), and there is an intriguing ambiguity about the fig- ures in the *Two Scholars Disputing* (Plate 2). Who are they? Are they really scholars? named Greek philosophers? Old Testament prophets, or New Testament saints? It has recently been suggested that they are the apostles Peter and Paul (though they lack their traditional at- tributes, the key and the sword). These things strike a new, arresting note.

About 1630 Rembrandt steps back a pace or two from the subject and places the figures in the second plane in a high vaulted space. Perhaps attracted by indirect knowledge of Caravaggio, he makes the observation of a pool of light sur- rounded by darkness the visual motive of the picture. Where there is only one figure, this figure is often represented in contemplation or asleep, so that the shadowy atmospheric space above appears as an emanation of thought or dreams. Visually it is as if Rembrandt were standing at a distance watching the light as it fell from a high window in a dim Gothic interior. Similar but not identical means are used for the depiction in this setting of a lonely scholar seated

15

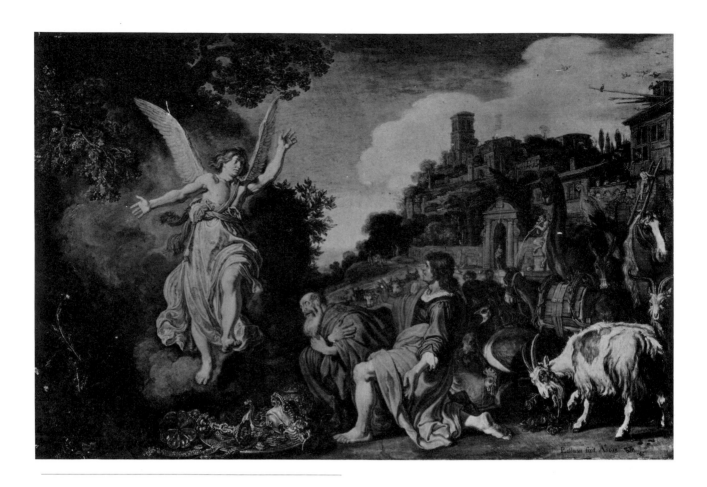

Fig. 4
PIETER LASTMAN
Tobit and Tobias Kneeling before the Angel

PANEL, 63 × 92 CM. SIGNED 'P. LASTMAN F. 1618'. COPENHAGEN,
STATENS MUSEUM FOR KUNST

by a window and the *Presentation of Jesus in the Temple* (Plate 7). The difference is that, whereas in the secular scene the light has a visible source, in the latter the natural light is fused with a supernatural radiance emanating from the figure group; yet this is done so subtly that we are only subconsciously aware of it and the way the light falls strikes us at first glance as natural. Rembrandt was to use this device again and again in religious pictures in the future.

The composition of the *Presentation* is ab-

solutely calm. No one moves or speaks but everyone looks. It is a picture about looking, about understanding through the eyes. In the central group, gazes are fastened on Simeon holding the Christ-Child; he returns them in the direction of the tall robed figure, whose profile is lost in shadow. Other figures — grave Rabbis seated in the foreground, a more excited crowd dimly visible on the steps to the right — watch from a distance. Two old men from the crowd have come forward to join the central group, peering over Mary's shoulder. We recognize in them the many pen and ink studies of beggars which Rembrandt made from life during this period. Thus is reality blended with sacred history. The solemn mood leaves us in no doubt that we, like the onlookers in the painting, are

16

witnesses to a divine revelation.

Within the scheme of light and shade, the composition is defined by lines: verticals in the figures and architecture, horizontals and receding diagonals along the steps and the divisions in the pavement. The vertical emphasis, which rises to a climax in the pillar to the right of centre, above the Infant Christ, rests on a firm base. The figures are also lineally conceived, but the lines fall as much within the forms, following the folds in drapery, as they do along their contours. We are again reminded of Rembrandt's drawings of this period, in which he used long looping strokes, hardly lifting his pen from the paper (Fig. 11). The colours are cool and close to one another in the spectrum; the brushwork is delicate and the surface smooth and luminous like deeply polished wood, echoing the wooden panel on which it is painted.

The Presentation in the Temple, executed in 1631 about the time that Rembrandt left Leyden for Amsterdam, is one of his first masterpieces on a small scale. But, regarding his career as a whole, we must take account not only of the intimate, closed, spiritual Rembrandt; there is also the open, monumental, baroque Rembrandt to be remembered. Perhaps initially the decision to work on a large scale was the desire to emulate Rubens, who deeply affected Rembrandt's art in the early 1630s and was, after Lastman, the most important single influence in his career. Rubens's richly plastic modelling, though not his composition, is already reflected in the heads of *The Anatomy Lesson of Dr Tulp* (1632; Plate 8), with which Rembrandt made his reputation on his arrival in Amsterdam. Like most of Rembrandt's group portraits this is partly a subject picture, since it contains an action and figures responding to it. The painting represents a private dissection, which would have preceded or followed the public one held by the surgeons' guild. Dr Tulp is shown demonstrating the muscles and tendons of the forearm and comparing his findings with a diagram in a recently published book on anatomy, which has been iden-

tified. Nevertheless, the composition is as much that of a group portrait as of a documentary record, and the action, in addition to being basically true to life, is a device for unifying the picture. What contemporaries would have admired is Rembrandt's virtuosity as an artist: his invention, the vividness of the expressions, his smooth brushwork and the skilful foreshortening of the naked corpse. In Amsterdam in 1632, this was what painting was supposed to be about.

Belshazzar's Feast (Plate 11), another large work of this decade which exhibits similar qualities, is still more ambitious. Whether it is equally successful is another question. Rembrandt, here unhampered by real life, gives his imagination free rein. It is a painting designed to impress. It displays difficult technical problems chosen and overcome: not only expression but lighting, movement and the treatment of exotic still-life accessories and costumes. Much is made of the play of both direct and reflected light on surfaces. This is especially true at the left, where the woman seated in the foreground seems literally bathed in phosphorescence. Softer, partly reflected light glances over the two figures facing Belshazzar, while another figure almost lost in shadow hovers dimly in the background. On the right a swaying, foreshortened figure reflects the influence of Venetian painting both in pose and in the painting of the red velvet sleeve. The composition is defined by powerful baroque diagonals anchored at the centre by the massive body of Belshazzar and focused on the great jewelled clasp of his cloak. The impasto is very thick and heavily worked in this area, as if mimicking the substance it is representing. The cloak, turban and trinkets would have been modelled on the bizarre costumes and curios with which Rembrandt stuffed his studio wardrobe.

This is perhaps Rembrandt's most purely theatrical painting. Everything in it is emphatic, exotic and astounding. Yet for most modern critics it is a failure. It seems to be too lacking in other qualities. The dramatic event which touches off the action — 'the Writing on the Wall' — is sensational enough to justify the rhetoric but we feel that Rembrandt is trying too hard. Wine spilling not just from one but from *two* goblets is too much. The expressions are overdone and the painting of Belshazzar's face and hands is ugly and grotesque. But it is at least — with some of the early self-portraits — a corrective to the sentimental view of Rembrandt. Only he could have carried off such a monstrous performance.

After this, Rembrandt progressively diminishes the area in which rich costumes and precious metals appear, yet until the last decade there is usually a hint of such richness somewhere in the picture, of brocades or burnished metals glowing like fire. Rhetoric also dies away and, from the early 1640s onwards, outflung arms and grimacing features — the outward, baroque means of conveying emotion — are replaced by subtle hints of feeling in the eyes, set of the head and pose.

The transition to a new kind of art was effected in a number of tranquil scenes painted during the 1640s, the common theme of which is domestic piety. We find this epitomized in the Old Testament (*The Departure of the Shunamite Woman; Tobit and Anna*) as well as in the New (*The Holy Family*, Plates 22 and 23, and *The Adoration of the Shepherds*). No mythological subjects were painted during this decade, even among the single figures. The most typical single figure is the impoverished, bearded old man, hatless or wearing a simple cap, seen head and shoulders only, and the young servant girl appearing at a window (Plate 21). Whether this withdrawal into a more intimate kind of art was occasioned by reaction (Rembrandt's, not his contemporaries') against the bombast of *The Night Watch* (1642; Plates 18 and 19), by grief at the death of his wife, or by factors in his own interior life, is uncertain. Rembrandt's own thoughts and feelings, as distinct from their manifestations in his appearance (as seen in his self-portraits) lie outside our knowledge.

Perhaps the most significant development — it is even more important than the subject and composition — consists in the technique. A simple way of putting this is to say that the brushwork becomes broader, but there is more to it than that. The change affects the whole treatment of form. An alternative explanation might be to suggest that the top layers of paint have been left off and that the surface now visible is what would previously have been the underpainting or a sketch; in other words, one might describe the paintings, as the early critics described them, as unfinished. In fact they are not unfinished, nor did Rembrandt simply substitute sketches for finished pictures. On the whole he did not make preparatory sketches in oil except for some of his early etchings. Nevertheless, the analogy with the sketch and the first stages of a painting is one way of understanding the process by which the new technique was achieved. A glance at the monochrome sketch of the *Entombment of Christ* (Plate 13) will illustrate this, as it shows what happens at its simplest and most extreme. Not only are the surfaces of the forms left out but the transitions between tones are omitted as well. A stroke of paint is used simultaneously to indicate the tone of a form and its approximate shape. Differing tones are placed side by side instead of being blended into one another. This brushwork is a kind of 'note form'. It is functional and without embellishments; it does not suggest movement or texture; it denotes rather than describes.

It could not be more different from the highly finished parts of earlier paintings, like the *Presentation in the Temple*. There the brushwork follows the contours and internal modelling of the forms, describing their surface minutely. The tones are blended, the stroke is soft and linear. This even applies to more vigorously handled works of the late 1630s, like *The Risen Christ Appearing to the Magdalene* (Plate 14). It is only in subsidiary parts of these paintings, which are not meant to attract the eye particularly and where the forms are slightly indistinct, that the simplified brushwork of the forties is anticipated. (Contrary to what might be expected, it does not seem to be anticipated in Rembrandt's most personal, and therefore most freely handled, early paintings, such as his portraits of himself and his wife; the brushwork in these is looser but its descriptive character is the same as that of other works of the period.)

However, in the 1640s there are differences as well as similarities in technique between Rembrandt's finished paintings and his sketches. For one thing, speed is of the essence in a sketch, and Rembrandt was not interested in speed; Baldinucci records that he was a slow worker, going over passages again and again, waiting for each layer to dry, until he was satisfied with the result. More important, the brushstrokes in the finished paintings of this period (e.g. *The Holy Family with Angels*, Plate 22) are very refined and their shapes are carefully calculated. Each touch is unobtrusive yet of the utmost significance. It conveys simultaneously form, colour, texture and tone. To some extent the last three could be adjusted later by means of glazes but the form had to be exactly right from the first; its shape had to be defined exactly by the mark made by the brush. In some of the figures in smaller works, a complete head or hand may be represented by a single brushstroke, without modulations of tone. No more than three or four strokes are required for the headcloth of the Madonna in *The Holy Family with Angels*; another single broad stroke suffices for the piece of this cloth which comes over her right shoulder (a similar economy of means is to be found in Rembrandt's drawings). In still later works (see the hands in the portrait of Jan Six, Fig. 33), proportionately fewer strokes are used for more complex forms. Nor are there many different tones in these forms. The main tonal variations are expressed by juxtaposition, not by blending. The slight changes which suggest the play of light and atmosphere over the forms are obtained by glazes. One advantage of this broader yet very precise method of handling was that Rembrandt

could make larger, seemingly 'empty' areas visually interesting. He could avoid the fussiness which characterizes many of his paintings of the previous decade, such as *The Risen Christ Appearing to the Magdalene* (Plate 14). What earlier or contemporary painter could have made so commonplace an object as a child's wicker cradle seem so fascinating to the eye? The paint has a beauty in itself, over and above its representational function.

The brushwork also had another purpose: to represent emotion. Rembrandt was no longer interested in conveying expression by exaggerated facial movements, that is to say, by movements which he could describe by tracing their outlines with the brush. He knew that human emotions are often expressed by only very slight changes in the facial muscles — perhaps only around the eyes and at the corners of the mouth — changes which the observer in real life is able to pick up but which are too subtle to be represented by conventional formulas of expression. By placing the brushstroke just 'so', in the cheek below the eye or along the eyelid, Rembrandt was able to record these tiny movements and hence to imply the expression in the eye itself. This gave him, further, the power to convey a whole range of emotions that were outside the capacity of previous artists. This applies particularly to the inward or contemplative emotions of love, compassion and apprehension, as distinct from the outgoing and active ones of terror and rage. In his middle and later years Rembrandt hardly ever represented figures in violent states of feeling. Moreover, his mastery of expression was not confined to the treatment of faces; it is also evident in his painting of hands and indeed the whole body. No painter has made so much of the touching of one figure by another with a hand: the husband laying a hand on his wife's shoulder in *Jupiter and Mercury Visiting Philemon and Baucis* (Plate 37); *Jacob Blessing the Children of Joseph* (Plate 35); Mary reaching out a hand to lift the cloth from the Child's cradle without waking Him (Plate 22).

The technical characteristics which have been discussed are epitomized in this last, most beautiful and most central painting of Rembrandt's middle years. To study it is to realize that what can be described as technique is not a dry mechanical dexterity but the counterpart of imaginative and spiritual qualities. Here is the familiar theme of the Madonna and Child represented in the costumes and setting of a *genre* scene (Goethe's 'Dutch peasant woman') but made sacred, not just by the presence of angels, but by the colour, expressions and brushwork. By keeping the colours and lighting very pure and by a slight emphasis on the regularity of certain forms — the line of Mary's shoulder, the oval of her face, the smoothness of her brow — Rembrandt invests the figure with a sweetness which proclaims that this is no ordinary mother but the Mother of God.

In Rembrandt's late art this sweetness is avoided. It is an art largely dominated by men: the Madonna hardly reappears; the characteristic female figure is the virtuous Roman matron, Lucretia, who stabbed herself in shame after being raped (Plate 48). Many of the paintings are large. The figures are almost all life-size and are usually shown in three-quarter length. The conception of the pictures is monumental and austere, although it may encompass moods both of great tenderness (*The Jewish Bride*, Plate 47) and bitter humiliation (*The Disgrace of Haman* in Leningrad). The sentiment in the second of these paintings is conveyed entirely through facial expression and is not even fully apparent to a spectator ignorant of the story. Equally, the late pictures may include a strain of vivid realism, as in the *Two Negroes* (Plate 44); or they may summon up ghosts. What apparitions are they, what survivors of some unknown Northern mythology, that gather round the table to swear the oath in *The Conspiracy of Julius Civilis* (Plate 38)?

However, we are more conscious of what unites the late works than of what divides them. The trend is away from realism and narrative, and towards essence rather than existence. Even the expressions are often mute or inscrutable; the figures think and feel but no longer communicate as before. They embody a kind of super-real presence which is all the more intense for being without corresponding form or rational cause. The observation of light and shade is less illusionistic than before. The brushwork also almost ceases to have a representational function and to become, instead, an independent medium. We often cannot tell the material of which the costumes are made. The paint, applied in square overlapping patches, layer upon layer, scratched with the handle of the brush, scraped off and reapplied, has its own extraordinary character, its own vitality. The marks scarcely define the shape of forms; like the penstrokes in the late drawings or the drypoint lines in the late etchings, they lie outside or within, not along, the contours. Blocked in with straight edges, they serve as lines of force, indicating direction.

The forms, though massive in area, are insubstantial and flattened, and limbs that would normally be seen in foreshortening are sometimes distorted in order to bring them into a plane parallel with the picture surface. The integrity of the picture surface is all. What we see is a tapestry of colours and tones into which figures and faces are dimly yet palpably woven. A greater number of different tones and different shades of the same or related colours, each distinct yet harmonized with the others, is visible than in the work of any other artist, not even excepting the late Titian. The effect is at once dream-like and intensely vivid; subtle and overpoweringly impressive. Like the late work of many other great artists, Rembrandt's is essentially tragic. As the mind contemplates it, it is purged of the emotions of pity and terror and brought to a state of peace.

The Portraits

In discussing Rembrandt's portraits it is difficult not to begin with the cliché that he was the greatest portrait painter of all time. This statement does not take us very far; and if true, it imposes an obligation on the critic to explain why it should be so. At all events, it will generally be agreed that Rembrandt embodies most of our ideas of what a great portrait painter should be. Nowadays we think more highly of that type of portraiture which reveals character than of that which reveals mere likeness. We expect a portrait to uncover 'the real man', to show him warts and all and to disclose the private weaknesses behind the public face. We would rather that the painter were the critic than the flatterer of his sitters. Further, we ask that a portrait should tell us as much about the artist as about the person portrayed; that it should be the product of a collaboration between the two, the end in view being the creation of a work of art.

Now, these are democratic expectations, which previous ages for the most part did not share. It happens that Rembrandt — in a sense — satisfies them; the fact that he does so is one reason for his popularity today. But Rembrandt fulfils the modern requirements of portraiture to both a greater and lesser extent than might be supposed. As usual, his method is not reducible to a formula; nor is it easy to group his portraits and single figures into categories for purposes of discussion. Although they all have some things in common, each turns out on examination to be a unique achievement.

The painting of a portrait poses two main artistic problems. The first, which applies to all representations of the single figure, is how to avoid monotony. It is one failing of the second-rate portrait painter that all his sitters, apart from their features and sometimes clothing, tend to look alike. Even the very good portrait painter of the second rank, like Frans Hals, may, by emphasizing the pose and introducing gestures and movement, achieve only a superficial variety, since if these factors are overstressed they appear contrived. Rembrandt generally keeps the poses of his sitters quiet and unassuming, although they are never dull, and he rarely uses gesture or movement. Except in his earliest self-portraits the expressions are also restrained, and this becomes increasingly true in his later work; there is always something withheld from, as well as given to, the observer. Rembrandt's chief means of gaining variety are firstly, the use of costumes and attitudes which show the sitter adopting a role (this is not confined to portraits of himself and his family, although it most clearly evident there); and secondly, the creation of a mood of introspection or internal drama, into which the observer finds himself drawn. This mood stimulates curiosity and produces a suggestion of 'content' which is like that of subject paintings, not just of portraits, and hence is capable of similar pictorial variations. By concentrating on the sitter's psychology, sometimes emphasizing one side of his personality by showing him acting a role, Rembrandt achieves a more genuine variety than he would have done if he had used more superficial means.

The second problem of portaiture is that of representing character. Ever since the Renaissance, it has been understood that the portrait painter has a duty to reveal the character of his sitters and not merely to copy their likeness. Until comparatively recently this did not mean probing the sitter's inner psychology; it was sufficient if his more salient virtues were displayed. The task presented no theoretical problem, since it was generally believed — following the basic premise of that popular intellectual game of the period, physiognomics — that 'the face is the index to the mind'. In practice, however, the achievement of this aim was very difficult, not so much because of the inherent limitations of the visual medium of painting, although these were serious enough, but because of a fallacy in the theory. Briefly, this fallacy was the assumption that it is possible to *deduce* a person's character from a painted image of his features, whereas in fact his character can only be *recognized* by this means; in other words, the face only reveals the qualities of a person's character to those who are aware of them already. To friends and contemporaries of the sitter, his portrait may reveal him 'to the life', but its doing so depends on their knowing him in life and being able to read into the portrait his typical expression, aspects of his character and so on, which are already familiar to them. To take a specialized case — one of the few recorded contemporary comments on Rembrandt as a portrait painter: the poet Vondel exhorted Rembrandt, when portraying Cornelisz. Claesz. Anslo (Fig. 5), who was a famous preacher in Amsterdam, 'to paint Cornelisz's voice'. Whether Vondel was satisfied with the result is not known, but Rembrandt's presumed success, even in the metaphorical sense in which Vondel meant it, is inevitably lost on us as we have no means of comparing the painting with the living model. It follows from this that a portrait can convey character to posterity to something like the extent it did to contemporaries only if the sitter is historically very well known; that is to say, if we possess written information about him which we can read into his portrait in the same way that contemporaries were able to apply their knowledge of him gained from life. Unfortunately none of Rembrandt's sitters is sufficiently well known in this sense.

It does not seem that the significance of this aspect of the problem of portraying character found a place in Renaissance and seventeenth-century art theory. Nevertheless, painters appear to have grasped it intuitively from an early date and to have attempted to convey certain elements of a sitter's character by means which posterity and those unacquainted with him in

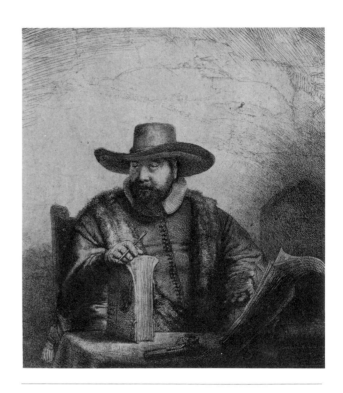

Fig. 5
Portrait of the Preacher, Cornelisz. Claesz. Anslo

ETCHING, 18.6 × 15.7 CM. SIGNED 'REMBRANDT F. 1641'. WEST BERLIN, KUPFERSTICHKABINETT

the flesh could discern (this is particularly evident in portraits of rulers, where the monarch's or prince's authority and virtues had to be conveyed to his or her subjects and to foreign powers). One favourite method was to include symbolic attributes of the sitter's accomplishments or profession; another was the use of emblems; a third was idealization of the sitter's features and body, to emphasize his position in society and distinction of mind. Rembrandt, as might be expected, had a deeper understanding of the problem than any other painter, yet he used hardly any of the usual, mostly external, devices. His means were chiefly inward-looking and subjective — above all, the *chiaroscuro*. He used *chiaroscuro* to create an appropriate mood or a revealing play of emotions in the sitter's features. Alternatively, he would emphasize some features at the expense of others; thus in some of his self-portraits he adjusts the shadow down one side of his face to hide the bulbousness of his nose. In this type of self-portrait he presents himself as refined and relaxed, quietly confident of his powers; in other types the thickness of his features is unsparingly revealed and he appears aggressive when young or anguished when old. A further means of expressing character, as it is of achieving variety, is also common in Rembrandt's portraits. This is the casting of the figure in some guise or role by the use of costumes, the pose and, occasionally, associations of style. At one extreme this takes the form of dressing up or play-acting, as in *Saskia as Flora* (Plate 9 and Fig. 12). At the other extreme it may appear as a subtle emphasis on one side of a sitter's personality at the expense of others: slight adjustments to the composition and *chiaroscuro* in the portrait of Jacob Trip (Plate 40) tend, without detracting from his individuality, to build him up into 'the man of authority'. In the same way, Rembrandt presents himself in his self-portraits now as 'the artist' (Plate 41), now as 'the gentleman' (Plate 15), and so on.

From all this it is evident that Rembrandt's depiction of character is far from being the total disclosure that it is sometimes made out to be (though it is significant that those who hold this view tend to be reticent as to the precise characteristics disclosed). What Rembrandt achieves is all that a painter can achieve, namely to show, by artistic means, certain qualities of a sitter's character that we might be able to recognize in his face if we knew him in life. It is in the nature of things that we cannot specify or label these qualities very exactly and that our understanding of them is subjective; yet, such is Rembrandt's skill, they can be identifed within fairly narrow limits. Beyond these limits, Rembrandt gives us 'character' in a more general sense, as we say in the phrase 'this figure is full of character', or that person is 'a man of character'.

He does this by making his figures look within themselves as well as out towards us, and by presenting them in a context of introspection and thought. These qualities will be discussed again in a moment but at this point it will be convenient to look at some examples of Rembrandt's portraiture in slightly more detail. They will be taken in approximate chronological order but the differences between them can be found at all stages of his career and only partly reflect a development in his approach.

The first is the enchanting *Saskia as Flora* in Leningrad of 1634 (Plate 9). This is a costume piece like the well-known painting of the same subject in London, but the two are not identical in treatment. In the London *Saskia* (Fig. 12) we are very much aware of the contrast between the sitter and her costume, although this contrast is itself revealing and not merely awkward. It is a portrait of Saskia unaccustomed to this fancy dress. In the Leningrad painting the sitter, though still clearly recognizable as Saskia, has been more fully assimilated to the idea of a classical goddess. The metamorphosis is not complete and is all the more touching for that, but Saskia's face is sweetened and she steps into her pastoral role with a grace that owes something to Titian and Rubens as well as to contemporary Dutch conventions of pastoral painting. Her pregnancy adds the idea of fertility to the traditional conception of the classical goddess of spring. The handling is smooth and the colours unusually clear and decorative for Rembrandt. Flowers appear in the background as well as in Saskia's hair and wound round her staff. The gesture of holding something lightly in the hand, as so often in Rembrandt, is an indication of informality; for example, Jan Six drawing on his gloves (Plate 32) or Titus puzzling over his homework (Plate 31). The picture sustains, fused and in perfect balance, a number of contrasting associations: those of reality, mythology and the stage. Is the figure Saskia dressed up as Flora, or an allegorical painting of Flora for which Saskia sat as a model? That the answer is in doubt is an index of the painting's position on the borderline between portraiture and mythology. It is at once a personal record of Rembrandt's affection for his wife — and hence it tells us something about one side of her personality — and a commentary on the pastoral convention of spring.

The treatment of the *Jacob Trip* (Plate 40) is very different. Here, every stroke proclaims the idea of authority — parallel verticals of the stick and the chair, the severely upright pose, the look in the heavy-lidded eyes, and the shadows which fall in such a way as apparently to lengthen the face. It happens that several other portraits of Trip by different artists are known, from which it can be seen that Rembrandt's is a good likeness. But the comparison also shows that it is very much more than a likeness. The versions by Cuyp and Maes tell us little more than that the sitter was an old man with a thin face and hooked nose. Rembrandt depicts the aged armaments manufacturer as a symbol of iron will-power. No Old Testament prophet or mythological sage elsewhere in his *œuvre* is as gaunt as this formidable ancient figure, who is both sinister and wise, a merchant patriarch of the new, Protestant Jerusalem which was Amsterdam. Even if the sitter's whole personality cannot be understood, if the presentation is one-sided, and though any interpretation is bound to be subjective, there is no doubt that this is an image of 'character'. And it is achieved by aesthetic means: by the low viewpoint and imposing breadth of the lower part of the figure, by the massive cloak and archaic, throne-like chair, and, most subtly, by the *chiaroscuro*. This elongates the face and figure, widens the forehead and enlarges the eyes.

The Falconer (Plate 43) is an equally impressive but more ambiguous work, at once tragic and flamboyant. Is it an imaginary historical portrait? a portrait of a character in a play? a painting of a model in invented clothes? Certainly it has a strange air of unreality: the horse, the groom, the bird — none of these look as if painted from life. Rembrandt seems here to

bring back the baroque or Venetian fancy picture in a new guise. The powerful face is pictorially integrated with the rest of the composition yet appears psychologically detached from it. The large eyes are the focus of the picture yet register a blank stare. The brushwork, like the conception as a whole, is broad and vigorous and comparatively unbroken for the late date. The colour — hot red, orange and gold throughout — plays a more independent role than in earlier works and establishes the painting's mood. The model is one who appears frequently in Rembrandt's art around 1660 in a number of different guises — as Christ, as an apostle or as an unnamed bearded man. It is characteristic that his features and age should be varied in each of these representations. Rembrandt's ability to paint from the life and yet alter what he sees is often overlooked by those who try to interpret his portraits and studies of single figures too literally. This is particularly true of his use of his mistress, Hendrickje (Plate 29), as a model. The question, when confronted with a painting of a young or young-ish woman, 'is it Hendrickje?', often does not admit of a clear yes or no answer.

Contemplation or introspection is the *leitmotiv* of Rembrandt's mature and late portraits. Sunk in reverie or gazing towards the observer, the figures seem to exist in an atmosphere of their own. They are watchful yet withdrawn, and behind the eyes the mind is preoccupied by thought. Rembrandt began treating portraits and studies of old people in this way very early in his career, then applied the same method to his self-portraits, and finally extended it to all his portraits in varying degrees after 1640. As a conception of portraiture this was not without precedents: the *Mona Lisa* is one famous example and there are others of a slightly different kind in the work of Titian. But Rembrandt developed this type of portrait further than anyone else and used it for a far wider range of sitters. Although its most typical representatives are men accustomed to thought rather than action — doctors, preachers and artists — it is not confined to them.

Rembrandt's principal means is once more the *chiaroscuro*. The face normally receives the strongest light, which gives it the prominence which its importance in the portrait leads one to expect. At the same time the face is criss-crossed by shadows which both lend it interest and character and enmesh it, as it were, in the background. Shadows collect in and around the eyes and the hollows of the cheeks, down one side of the nose and round the mouth. Sometimes the eyes are heavily shaded by a hat. The edges where one tone meets another are softened, and it is frequently the side of the face turned towards the observer which is illuminated, thereby avoiding a sharply silhouetted cheek-line on the other side. The effect of all this is to divert attention from the face as a unit and transfer it to the features. The features, especially the eyes, thus become all the more telling as indicators of mood and character. Yet for all their rich expressiveness they remain partly inscrutable, for two reasons. The first reason is that the eyes are defined by the shadows, not by the light, which gives them a far-away look, as if there were some invisible force uniting them with the background (it is remarkable how much more aggressive — and less interesting — the faces in Rembrandt's portraits appear if they are looked at with the backgrounds masked off). The second reason is that the expressions are not superficially animated. Rembrandt's sitters may watch the observer intently; they do not communicate with him. Their eyes are steady and their mouths closed. Animation lies in the technique — the fluid *impasto*, the delicate and varied glazing, the play of atmosphere and light and shade over the features; it does not lie in the features themselves.

This is a conception of portraiture that belongs at the opposite pole from arrested movement; the impression is rather one of immobility and timelessness. It follows that Rembrandt's portraits stand not just for the likeness and characterization of individuals. Nor do they add up to 'the portrait of an epoch'; they are not social documents. While each portrait is unique and each records the lineaments of a particular person, it carries overtones which make the individual the representative of suffering humanity. At bottom what Rembrandt portrays is the human predicament. And he saw that predicament as both tragic and watched over by a mysterious spiritual force. It is not for nothing that critics have seen a resemblance between Rembrandt's paintings and the philosophical ideas of his fellow resident of Amsterdam, Spinoza (although the latter was too young to have influenced him). Both men were steeped in the Jewish scriptures, and Rembrandt would have shared Spinoza's doctrine of the integration of spirit and matter. The mystery which permeates Rembrandt's shadows is ultimately a metaphor of the immanence of God.

There is one further characteristic of Rembrandt's portraiture: the intensity of the relationship between the sitter and the observer. Although in one sense Rembrandt's sitters are remote from us, in another sense they are vividly real. They are vulnerable to scrutiny and, wearing no social mask, they draw us into their world. The experience of looking at them is essentially private; it excludes the presence of a third person and exposes the observer to his own thoughts and feelings as much as it reveals those of the person portrayed (contrast Frans Hals, whose sitters often seem to be looking over the observer's shoulder at someone else). There is some reason to believe that Rembrandt always wanted his paintings to be contemplated very intimately. He interposed first the background, then the frame, as a barrier between the painted image and the outside world — this was the reverse of the baroque principle of extending the created world of the painting into the observer's space. In two cases, not portraits (one is *The Anatomy Lesson of Doctor Joan Deyman*; Plate 36), Rembrandt indicated the type of frame he would like: it was a kind of tabernacle, with pilasters either side, a base and a curved or pedimented top. In a third example, *The Holy Family with a Cat* (Plate 23), such a frame, together with a curtain half drawn in front of the scene, actually forms part of the picture.

To be exact, the contemplation of Rembrandt's portraits usually involves three people: the sitter, the observer and the artist. But there was one category in which this number was reduced to two: the self-portraits. Perhaps it is not altogether fanciful to see this factor as an additional, aesthetic reason, over and above the personal and autobiographical ones, for the quantity of self-portraits in Rembrandt's *œuvre*. In the self-portrait he was able to address the observer directly, without the distraction of another personality. If a portrait becomes a work of art as the result of a collaboration between the sitter and the artist, that collaboration is most effective when sitter and artist are one. When painting himself Rembrandt was freer to vary his interpretation by adopting a wider range of poses, costumes and lighting effects than he could use in his commissioned portraits; he could treat himself as either sitter or model, that is, he could depict himself either more or less formally; and, knowing himself better than he knew anyone else, he could make the self-por-

trait a more effective vehicle of character. He was sufficiently self-absorbed to represent his own features at least twice a year during his early and late periods (though less often, for some unknown reason, during his middle years), and he did so for the most part not in the casual or experimental media of drawings and oil sketches but in finished paintings and, to a lesser extent, etchings. Some of these painted self-portraits are as highly wrought as any portraits in his *œuvre*. It is not impossible that there was a market for them (significantly, not one is listed in the inventory of his possessions drawn up in 1656, although some of his less formal self-portraits may appear there disguised as *tronies* — 'heads'). If Rembrandt's self-portraits constitute a diary, as in a sense they do, it was a diary at least partly intended for publication.

Nevertheless, his self-absorption was accompanied by a remarkable objectivity. In his youth he was bold enough not to disguise his conceit; in his maturity and old age he became his own severest critic. To call Rembrandt's self-portraits his greatest achievement would be to fall into the trap of sentimentalizing him. It would also be incorrect. But they are in some ways the purest expression of his approach to portraiture.

A Note on the Landscapes

As we have seen, Rembrandt was not a *genre* painter, although he made many drawings of scenes from everyday life. It would be impossible to deny that he was a landscape painter, but the same distinction applies; that is, he made numerous landscape drawings from nature but very few naturalistic landscape paintings. Those exceptions apart, all his landscape paintings were imaginary, and they were all executed, in-

cluding the naturalistic ones (Plate 25), during his middle period, between about 1636 and 1655. As with his treatment of everyday life, the gap between his drawings and paintings was bridged by his etchings, which are partly naturalistic and partly verging on the imaginary.

Objectively it is hard to understand the gulf between the two categories. As a landscape draughtsman from nature (Fig. 6), Rembrandt was one of the most brilliant and inventive of all artists; light and air vibrate between every stroke of his rapid sketches of the open Dutch countryside. Rembrandt's paintings, on the other hand, are motionless and claustrophobic, despite their romantic intensity (Plate 17). To a greater extent than any of Rembrandt's other works they fall into a category of their own in the history of art. Whereas his subject pictures, painted figure studies and portraits entered the mainstream of later European painting, his landscape paintings have had only an occasional influence (for example, on English watercolours around 1800). Rembrandt's landscapes seem to deny one of the basic principles of the art: interest in the mutually supporting roles of space, light and air. Instead, these elements tend to contradict one another in his work. While the arbitrary relationship between the light and shade pattern and the composition is an effective source of visual surprise, it prevents the landscape from expanding outwards to the sides or backwards into depth as far as the horizon. The exceptions to this tendency prove the rule, for they occur not in his imaginary landscapes proper but in the background of a figure painting – *The Risen Christ Appearing to the Magdalene* (Plate 14) — and in the naturalistic *Winter Landscape* (Plate

25). Here, at least, the rendering of nature is beautifully fresh.

Yet Rembrandt's landscape paintings may become more intelligible if they are seen in the context of his own aesthetic attitudes. Like his ideas of architecture and costume, he evolved his conception of landscape independently of the classical tradition, that is, independently of the conventions of ideal landscape painting. Rembrandt's antiquity is an imaginary Hebraic antiquity, developed as an alternative to the Greek and Roman antiquity of Italian and Italianizing artists. Almost the only thing his landscapes have in common with ideal landscapes is that they are not naturalistic. But unlike ideal landscapes, and unlike the landscapes of that other great Northern inventor of imaginary scenes — Rubens — Rembrandt's landscape paintings have no real basis in the study of nature. Nor, unlike his drawings, are they Dutch in topography, although they show some Dutch stylistic influences. As was the case with his treatment of *genre* scenes, he transposed the subject-matter of his landscapes — nature — on to the plane of religious art. They have that brooding, numinous quality which informs so much of his work. They confirm once more, if only negatively, that the true subject of Rembrandt's art is man.

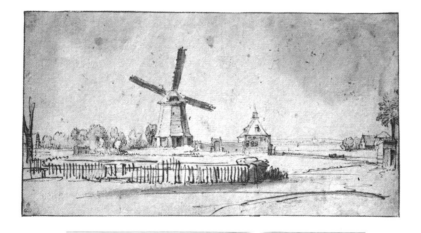

Fig. 6   Landscape with a Windmill

PEN AND BROWN WASH, 13.6 × 25.6 CM. C.1651. VIENNA, ALBERTINA

27

Outline Biography

1606 Rembrandt Harmensz van Rijn born on 15 July at Leyden, the son of Harmen Gerritsz. van Rijn, miller, and Neeltgen Willemsdochter van Zuidbroeck, daughter of a baker; the last but one in a family of seven.

1620 20 May: Rembrandt enrolled at Leyden University. His short stay there was presumably preceded by about 7 years spent in the Latin School at Leyden.

1620–5 Period of apprenticeship: three years with Jacob Isaaksz. van Swanenburgh in Leyden; six months with Pieter Lastman in Amsterdam (1624–5); perhaps also a short time with Jacob Pynas.

1625 Rembrandt returns to Leyden and sets up as an independent painter, sharing a studio with Jan Lievens (1607–74), also a former pupil of Lastman.

1628 February: Gerrit Dou (1613–75) becomes Rembrandt's first pupil, remaining with him perhaps until 1631/2.

1630 Death of Rembrandt's father.

1631/2 Between 8 March 1631 and 26 July 1632, Rembrandt settles permanently in Amsterdam, lodging first with the dealer, Hendrik van Uylenburgh, in the Breestraat.

1633 5 June: betrothal to Saskia van Uylenburgh (1612–42), the daughter of a former burgomaster of Leeuwarden and a cousin of Hendrik van Uylenburgh.

1634 22 June: marriage to Saskia at Sint-Annaparochie, near Leeuwarden.

1635 15 December: baptism of Rembrandt's and Saskia's first child, Rumbartus (buried 15 February 1636).

1638 22 July: baptism of a second child, Cornelia, called Cornelia I (buried 13 August 1638).

1639 12 January: Rembrandt is recorded as living in the Sugar Refinery on the Binnen Amstel. On 1 May he moves into a grand house, for which he is unable to pay in full, in the Breestraat.

1640 29 July: baptism of a third child, called Cornelia II (buried 12 August 1640). On 14 September, Rembrandt's mother is buried in St Peter's Church, Leyden.

1641 22 September: baptism of Rembrandt's and Saskia's fourth and only surviving child, Titus.

1642 14 June: death of Saskia.

1649 1 October: first reference to Hendrickje Stoffels (c.1625–63) as living in Rembrandt's household.

1654 30 October: baptism of Hendrickje's child, Cornelia.

1656 17 May: Rembrandt transfers the legal ownership of his house to Titus. 25 and 26 July: inventory of the contents of his house in the Breestraat drawn up by the Court of Insolvency. His appeal for the liquidation of his property, to avoid being declared a bankrupt, had been agreed shortly before.

1657 December: first sale of Rembrandt's possessions.

1658 1 February: the house in the Breestraat auctioned for 11,218 guilders (nearly 2,000 guilders less than Rembrandt had paid in 1639), although for legal reasons Rembrandt probably continued to live there until 1660. 14 February: further sale of possessions authorized. 24 September: final sale authorized of remaining prints and drawings in Rembrandt's collection, including many of his own (total, 600 guilders).

1660 Rembrandt moves to a smaller house in the Rozengracht. Titus and Hendrickje form a company for dealing in works of art, with Rembrandt as their employee.

1663 24 July: burial of Hendrickje Stoffels in the Westerkerk.

1668 10 February: marriage of Titus to Magdalena van Loo. On 7 September Titus is buried in the Westerkerk. A daughter, Titia, is born to Magdalena and baptized on 22 March 1669.

1669 4 October: Rembrandt dies in his house in the Rozengracht. He is buried in the Westerkerk, Amsterdam, on 8 October.

List of Illustrations

Colour Plates

Text Figures

Comparative Figures

1

Anna Accused by Tobit of Stealing the Kid

PANEL, 39.5 × 30 CM. SIGNED 'RHL 1626'. AMSTERDAM, RIJKSMUSEUM (THYSSEN BEQUEST)

The subject is taken from the Apocryphal Book of Tobit, Chapter II, vv. 11–14. Tobit was a wealthy, God-fearing Jew, strict in his observance of the Mosaic law, who had lost all his money and had been blinded in an accident. To keep them from starving, his wife Anna took in sewing and washing. One day, hearing the bleating of a kid which Anna had been given as a present to supplement her earnings, Tobit falsely accuses her of having stolen it. In return, she upbraids him for his self-righteousness which has brought them to their present plight (this is the scene represented in the picture). Later, however, the couple's fortunes are restored by their son, Tobias, who goes to find the money his father has lost and to marry a rich wife. On the way he meets the Angel Raphael, who instructs him when they come to a river to catch a large fish, the entrails of which are afterwards applied to Tobit's eyes to cure his blindness.

The scene of Tobias and the Angel journeying through the wilderness after finding the fish was very often represented in art throughout Europe. Dutch artists, however, were interested not only in that episode but in the whole Book of Tobit, which could be regarded both as picturesque and as an illustration of the workings of divine providence: though misfortunes occur, God will look after those who are obedient to his law. The fact that the story dealt with a family and with the devotion of a son to his father would have been an added attraction in a society which prized the domestic virtues. Tobit and Tobias kneeling before the Angel, showing their gratitude to God after Tobit had recovered his sight, was represented by Rembrandt's teacher, Lastman (Fig. 4), and Rembrandt himself painted the next moment in the story, the Angel leaving the family of Tobias, in a dramatic picture of 1637 now in the Louvre. For the composition of *Anna Accused by Tobit of Stealing the Kid*, he made use of an engraving after a picture by one of his recent predecessors, Willem Buytewech (see E. Havercamp Begemann, *Willem Buytewech*, Amsterdam, 1959, Fig. 126).

Rembrandt's lifelong fascination with old people is already evident in this painting, which dates from shortly after he had set up as an independent artist in Leyden in 1625. He was attracted by the lines in their faces and hands and by the very lack of elegance in their bodies, qualities which gave him the opportunity to display his mastery of detail and his skill with the brush. The brushstrokes are so smooth as hardly to be separately visible. Every surface and every drapery fold is carefully modelled in light and shade and, in contrast to his work of only a few years later, no contour line is lost. The colours are warm, pale and bright and the lighting is relatively even. The space depicted is confined but packed with domestic detail: onions hanging up by the window, a basket on the wall, cooking utensils on the shelves, part of Anna's sewing apparatus glimpsed between the two figures, and, in the foreground, Tobit's stick, his dog and a modest fire.

Such meticulously painted still-life detail had been a characteristic of Netherlandish art since the time of Jan van Eyck, if not earlier. However, in contrast to so many examples of its use up to and including the seventeenth century, it appears here to be without ulterior symbolic meaning. Like the expressions on the faces of the two figures and the gestures of their hands, its purpose is to give the maximum reality to the events of the story.

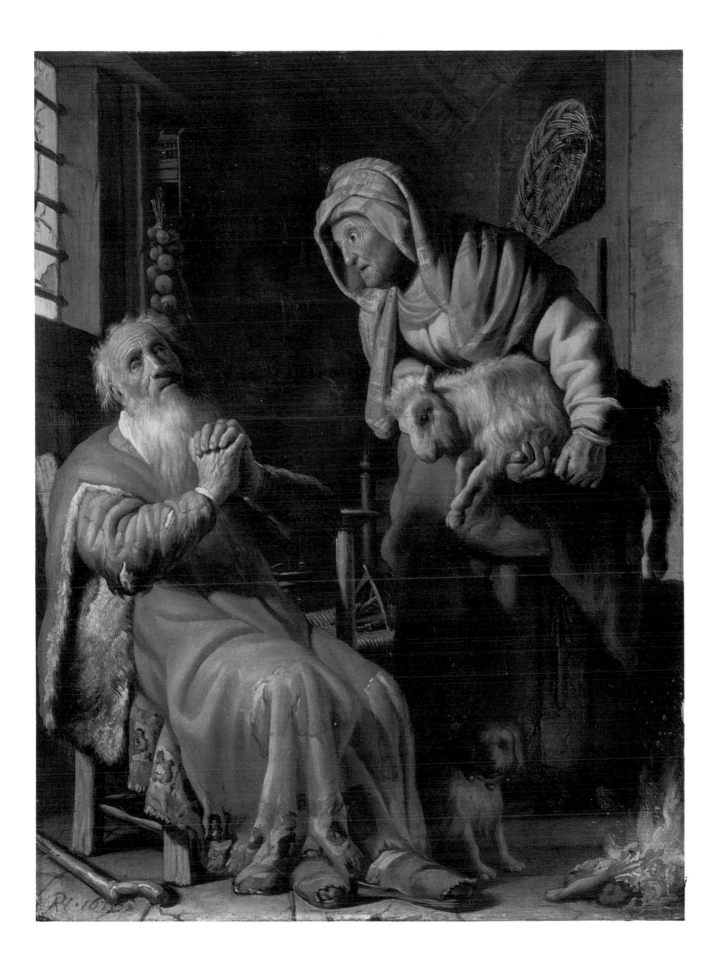

Two Scholars Disputing (St Peter and St Paul in Conversation?)

PANEL, 72.4 × 59.7 CM. SIGNED 'RHL 1628'. MELBOURNE, NATIONAL GALLERY OF VICTORIA, FELTON BEQUEST 1934

This is another typical small-scale work of Rembrandt's Leyden period, though now, two years after *Anna Accused by Tobit of Stealing the Kid* (Plate 1), the tone contrasts have become stronger and the forms more fluent and more powerful. The composition is defined by lines which move into the depth of the picture as well as forming a pattern on the surface, and it may not be an accident that 1628 is the first year from which drawings by Rembrandt survive in significant numbers; a spirited chalk study exists for the man in 'lost profile' on the left (Ben. 7).

The picture is probably that listed in an inventory, dated 1641, of the possessions of Rembrandt's patron and fellow artist, Jacob de Gheyn III (1596–1644), where it is described as 'Two old men disputing ... there comes the sunlight in.' The fact that it was not given a more specific title is not unusual (see also under Plate 5) and does not mean that Rembrandt had no specific subject in mind. Perhaps the true subject was unknown to whoever drew up the inventory, or was considered unimportant, or the compiler may have thought that the visual components of the picture gave a better description of it than a reference to its somewhat obscure subject-matter. The question of the subjects of Rembrandt's early works (and some of the later ones too) is indeed often quite difficult. If some contemporaries ignored or failed to recognize them, others attached titles to works where they were clearly inappropriate. This was the case with the Parisian print-publisher, Ciartres, who in the 1630s issued a series of engraved copies of Rembrandt's early etchings of warriors, orientals, etc., giving them fancy names like 'Mohammed' and 'Scandrebec, King of Albania'.

Assuming that Rembrandt intended the *Two Scholars Disputing* to be more than merely a *genre* scene, the most likely explanation is that it is *St Peter and St Paul in Conversation*, as has been suggested by Christian Tümpel ('Studien zur Ikonographie der Historien Rembrandts', *Nederlands Kunsthistorisch Jaarboek*, XX, 1969, pp. 107–98). Tümpel has demonstrated that there were several earlier representations of this theme in art (including one in particular by Lucas van Leyden) which show the two apostles as bearded scholars seated together, with one expounding a passage in a sacred book which the other holds on his knee. (The allusion is to St Peter's instruction of St Paul after the latter's conversion, mentioned in Galatians, Chapter I, v. 18: 'Then after three years I went up to Jerusalem to see Peter, and abode with him fifteen days.') Still, there is a considerable gap between these earlier representations and Rembrandt's picture. In the former, the two figures are invariably shown in a landscape, whereas Rembrandt, more logically, sets them in a scholar's study. More important, he omits the attributes – the key for St Peter and the sword and the book for St Paul – by which they were previously, and in art traditionally, identified. He relies only on the apostles' physical characteristics, as established by artistic precedent, and on what they are seen to be doing, that is earnestly discussing a text which the one (St Peter) is explaining to the other. Could this mean that Rembrandt was merely borrowing the pictorial motif and not taking over the biblical subject? Probably not, in fact, and there are many other instances among his paintings, together with still more among his drawings, in which he disdains the use of obvious – and artificial – recognition signs and represents the religious or mythological scene 'as it might really have happened'. It is worth noting, however, that ambiguities of the sort that arise here are less often to be found among his etchings, which were designed to reach a wider audience than his work in other media.

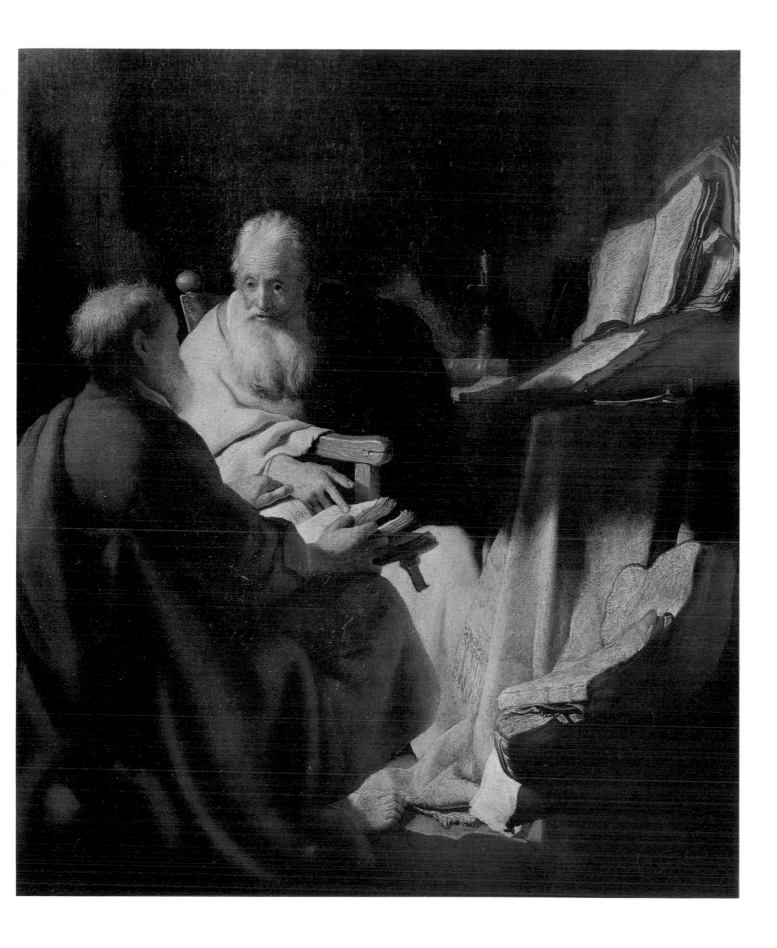

3

Self-Portrait (?)

PANEL, 41.2 × 33.8 CM. SIGNED WITH AN UNUSUAL MONOGRAM. C.1629–30. AMSTERDAM, RIJKSMUSEUM

Rembrandt began making paintings, drawings and etchings of himself in or about 1628, thereby inaugurating a career as a self-portraitist which is unique in the history of art. Those produced up to about 1631, when he moved to Amsterdam, form a distinct group. The majority – about fifteen – are etchings. Most, like the etching illustrated at the front of this book (Fig. 1), and the painting opposite, are not finished self-portraits in the ordinary sense but studies in expression. Moreover, by comparison with other self-portraits, including some of his own later ones, they are unusually direct in approach, sketch-like in execution and small in size. In part, Rembrandt was using them for practice, to discover for himself the range of expressions of which the human face is capable; he needed this information for the depiction of emotion in his subject pictures. In part, however, he was making use of a type of picture – the head-and-shoulders figure marked by a strong facial expression (the contemporary Dutch word is *tronie*) – popular in the Netherlands in the 1620s. Frans Hals's boldly painted studies of smiling children and Brouwer's heads of peasants, both produced in Haarlem, are characteristic examples. A variant of the type, often half-length, representing lute-players, singers or drinkers, occurs in the work of the Utrecht School. Where Rembrandt was original was in using his own features for this purpose.

The '*Self-Portrait*' reproduced here has been dated about 1629–30. However, the face seems uncharacteristically long for Rembrandt and the expression, like the monogram at the top right of the panel, is unusual; in most of the early self-portraits – drawings and etchings as well as paintings – the eyes are wide open, whatever the mouth may be doing. These qualities have given rise to doubts as to whether this painting represents the artist or, indeed, whether it is by Rembrandt. His early painted 'heads' were often imitated, and it is possible that this is an example. It does, however, represent the type which Rembrandt created very well.

It should be noted that Rembrandt, whether at this time of his life or at any other, did not always depict himself in an unflattering light. In the etched head, continued with black chalk, illustrated here as Figure 7, which he executed shortly before his move to Amsterdam, he shows himself as a tough-minded, arrogant and fashionably dressed young man, conscious of being on the threshold of success.

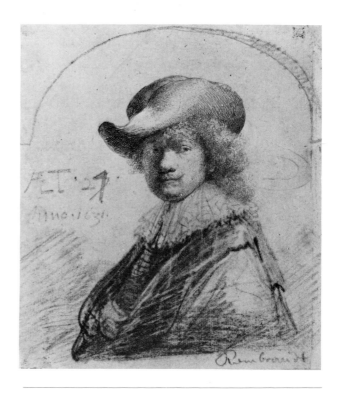

Fig. 7
Self-Portrait Aged Twenty-Four

ETCHING (HEAD ONLY), CONTINUED IN BLACK CHALK, 14.6 × 13 CM. SIGNED 'REMBRANDT' AND DATED, 1631. LONDON, BRITISH MUSEUM

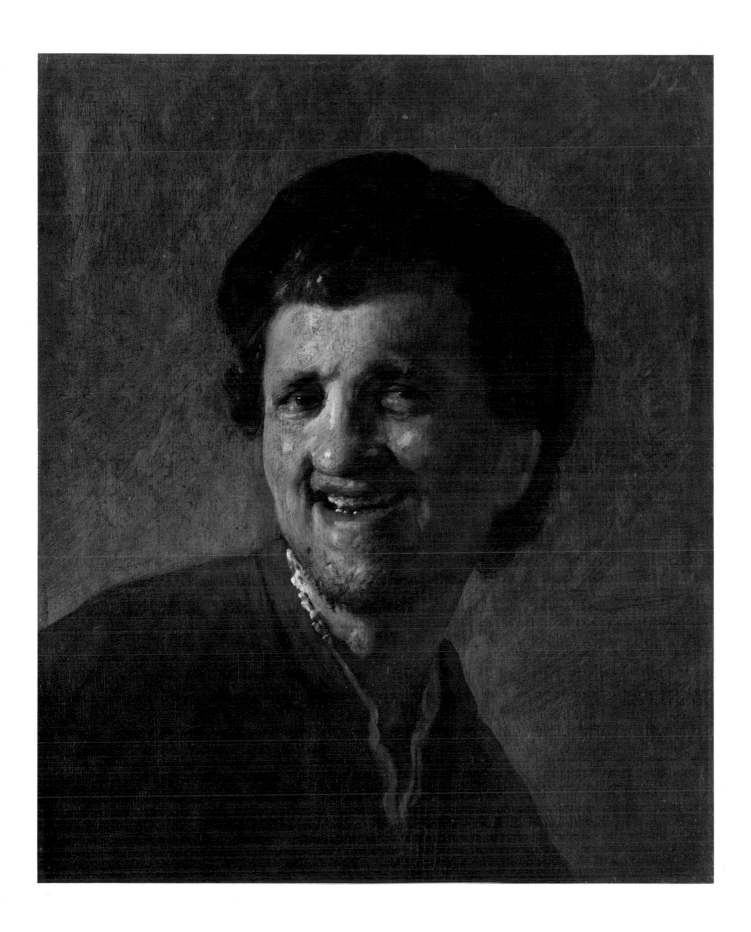

4

The Artist in his Studio

PANEL, 25 × 31.5 CM. C.1628–30. COURTESY, MUSEUM OF FINE ARTS, BOSTON

The theme of the artist in his studio was a popular one in seventeenth-century Dutch art, and Rembrandt returned to it several times in his drawings and etchings, though not again in his paintings (apart from his self-portraits holding palette and brushes, like Plate 41). On each occassion he did something original with it. Even in this early example, datable to about 1628–30, the image is very striking. In contrast to most Dutch artists who made of the theme a sumptuous, or at least cluttered, *genre* scene, Rembrandt depicts a bare room with the plaster cracked and peeling from its walls and with a large panel on the easel, its back evocatively turned towards the spectator. Several feet away from this, the tiny artist stands muffled in a long winter coat and wearing a hat, as if literally posing for his picture.

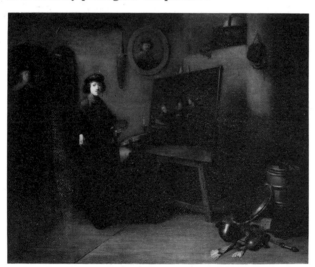

Fig. 8
GERRIT DOU
Rembrandt in his Studio

PANEL, 53 × 64.5 CM. 1628–30. PRIVATE COLLECTION

It is interesting to compare this painting with an almost contemporary representation of a similar, or perhaps even the same, scene by Gerrit Dou, who joined Rembrandt as his first pupil at the age of fourteen in February, 1628 (Fig. 8). So small is the artist in the Boston picture that it has been supposed that it is Dou, not Rembrandt, who is represented. Yet a comparison of the features with those of Rembrandt's early self-portraits, particularly a drawing in the British Museum (Ben. 53), shows that the figure is indeed that of the older artist. Moreover, the only other authentic full-length self-portrait by Rembrandt, a drawing made when he was about fifty (Fig. 30), indicates that he was a short, stocky man.

Dou's painting, which dates from about 1630, also depicts Rembrandt, though very differently. Now he appears as serious, elegant and almost deferential, and, as if to point the contrast, on the wall there is a typically aggressive *Self-Portrait* – not corresponding exactly to any of the known ones but similar to those in Stockholm and Liverpool (Br. 11–12). On the easel, this time facing the spectator, is an unidentified biblical scene, also lost, similar to the *Judas Returning the Thirty Pieces of Silver* (English Private Collection; Br.539A), which Huygens admired on his visit to Rembrandt in 1629. Various studio props, among them a bow, a parasol, a globe and a shield and helmet (the last two of which reappear in other paintings by both Rembrandt and Dou), are disposed about the room, and a visitor comes in at the door. In short, this is a 'public' picture of the artist, whereas Rembrandt's is a private one. Perhaps neither painter recorded the studio exactly as it was, and the truth may have lain somewhere between the two. As might be expected, Dou's picture reflects the influence of Rembrandt's style of this or perhaps a slightly earlier period, but already shows that extreme smoothness which was to remain the hallmark of his work throughout his life, which he lived out in Leyden.

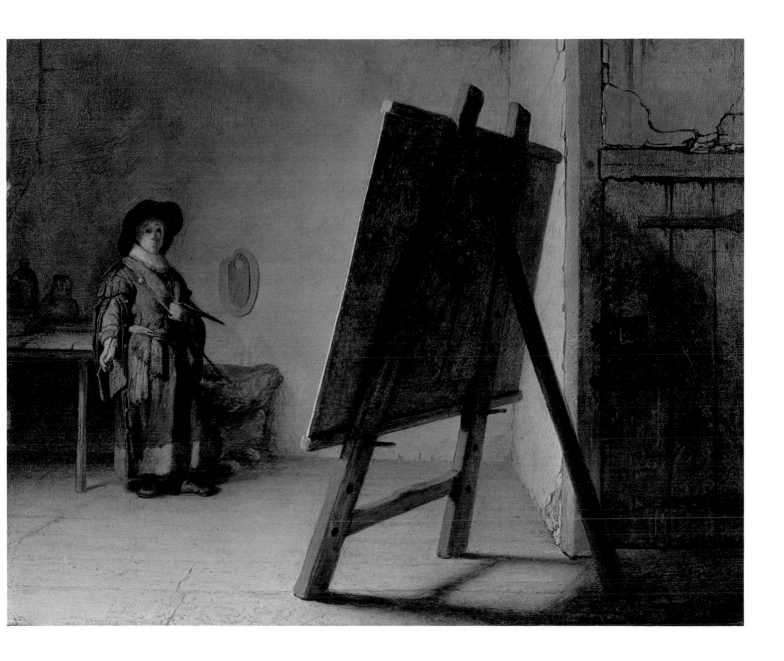

When the painting by Rembrandt was first discovered in the 1920s, it had a piece about 9 cm. high added to the panel at the top and a further 3 cm. added at the bottom. These were then cut off and thrown away as it was assumed that they were of later date. However, in 1964 it was plausibly argued by Seymour Slive in *The Burlington Magazine*, CVI, pp. 483–6, that the additions were by Rembrandt himself, although (in contrast to Rubens) he did not usually add to his panels in this way; an old photo-graph taken before the removal of the two pieces is reproduced in Slive's article. The larger size and upright format certainly agrees better with Rembrandt's style at this period, when he was beginning to open up the space of his compositions, and a drawing of an artist at an easel (Ben. 390), though somewhat later and not directly related to this painting, supports this view. However, the suggestion has not been universally accepted.

5

An Old Woman Wearing a Black Head-Scarf

PANEL, 61 × 47 CM. C.1629. ROYAL COLLECTION, WINDSOR CASTLE (REPRODUCED BY GRACIOUS PERMISSION OF HER MAJESTY THE QUEEN)

This is one of three pictures by Rembrandt presented to King Charles I by Sir Robert Ker, later Earl of Ancram, who probably acquired them in 1629 when he was on a diplomatic mission to The Hague; he may well have been given them by the Stadholder, Prince Frederick-Henry, or his Secretary, Constantin Huygens, rather than have purchased them directly from the artist. They were almost certainly the earliest of Rembrandt's paintings to leave The Netherlands and were the first to arrive in Britain. All three are likely to have been very recent works, and this is unquestionably true of the *Old Woman Wearing a Black Head-Scarf*, which cannot be eárlier than 1629 on stylistic grounds. According to an inscription on the back of the panel, it was given to Charles I 'by Sir Robert Ker', that is, before 1633 when he received his earldom. It is listed in Abraham van der Doort's catalogue of Charles I's collection, which was compiled in about 1638, as hanging in the Long Gallery at Whitehall Palace: 'Done by Rembrandt & given to the kinge by my Lo: Ankrom: Item ... an old woeman with a greate Scarfe upon her heade with a peaked falling band / In a Black frame' (see O. Millar, 'Abraham van der Doort's Catalogue of the Collections of Charles I', *The Walpole Society*, XXXVII, 1960, p. 60). The picture was sold in 1651 (listed as 'An old womans head – £4') by order of the Commonwealth but was recovered for the Royal Collection at the Restoration in 1660 (O. Millar, 'The Inventories and Valuations of the King's Goods, 1649–1651', *The Walpole Society*, XLIII, 1972, p. 265).

It is interesting that contemporaries described it as a *genre* painting, not a religious picture or a portrait (cf. the note to Plate 2). Until very recently, it was often thought to depict the artist's mother, who was married in 1589 and died in 1640, and this seemed to be borne out by the fact that etchings described as 'Rembrandt's mother' were listed in 1679 in the inventory of the art dealer, Clement de Jonghe, whose portrait was also etched by Rembrandt. However, in 1629, when the present picture was painted, Rembrandt's mother cannot have been more than sixty, whereas the figure here, even allowing for the comparative rapidity with which people aged in the seventeenth century, appears to be about eighty. The same woman is represented in other pictures and etchings by Rembrandt of this period, and she appears in paintings by Dou both before and after 1631, when Rembrandt moved to Amsterdam. It is therefore likely that she was an aged Leyden woman whom both artists used as a model. In at least one authentic painting by Rembrandt, that in the Rijksmuseum dated 1631 (Br. 69), where she is dressed in a dark red and gold head-cloth and reddish-brown fur cloak, she is shown reading a large sacred book. Because of this, she has been said to represent there the Prophetess Anna, and some traces of this identification may cling by association to paintings like the Windsor *Old Woman Wearing a Black Head-Scarf*. However, the distinction in these cases between a religious picture and a *genre* painting may not have been entirely clear even in Rembrandt's own mind.

Figure 9 is an example of the type of red chalk drawing from the life that Rembrandt made at about this time.

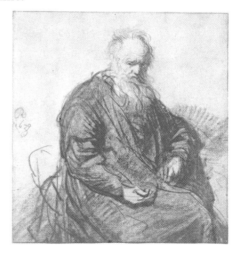

Fig. 9
A Seated Old Man

RED CHALK, 15.7 × 14.7 CM. SIGNED WITH INITIAL AND DATED, 1630. PRIVATE COLLECTION

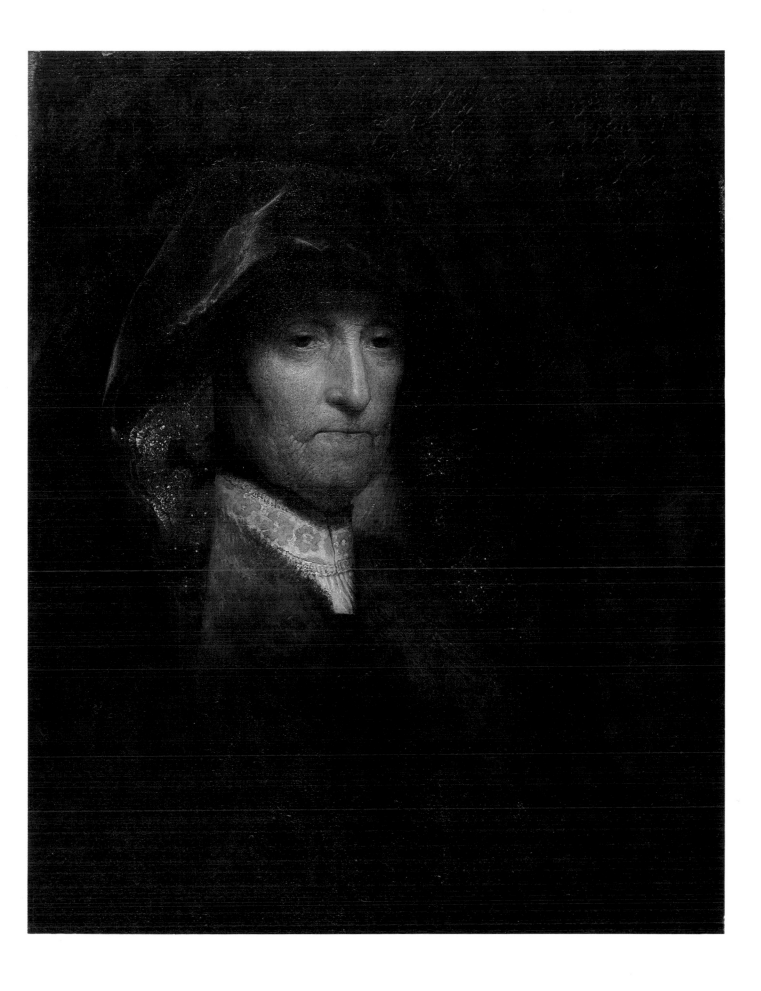

An Officer (?)

PANEL, 65 × 51 CM. SIGNED 'REMBRANDT F'. C.1630. PRIVATE COLLECTION

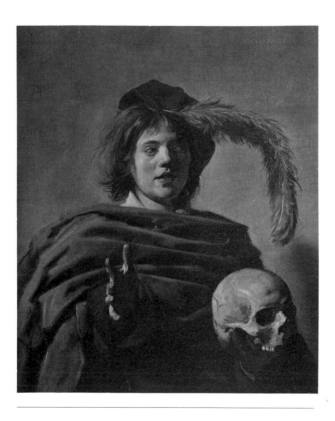

Fig. 10
FRANS HALS
A Young Man Holding a Skull

CANVAS, 92.2 × 80.8 CM. 1626–8. LONDON, NATIONAL GALLERY

This elderly, but not old, man with a large hooked nose, beady eyes and short beard is another figure who occurs several times in Rembrandt's early paintings and etchings. Like the old woman depicted in Plate 5, he has been identified with a relative of the artist: in this case, Rembrandt's father, who died in 1630. However, the justification on this occasion is even less, as the same man appears in a painting (Br. 82) and etching (M. 46) dated 1631. As with the old woman, not only his clothes but also his features vary slightly from picture to picture, revealing Rembrandt's ability to create something fresh with each new work. In some examples, the man wears a rather shabby fur garment and cap, but more often he is shown, as here, with a steel gorget round his throat and a feathered hat. Other accoutrements he sports in one painting or another are ear-rings and a gold chain with a pendant. If the gorget is intended to identify him as an army officer, he is a fierce, hard-bitten type, very different from the elegant cavaliers habitually painted by Frans Hals. One can imagine him as a soldier actually returned from the wars rather than a civilian dressed up in uniform for a social occasion.

Comparison may be made with Hals's *Young Man Holding a Skull* (Fig. 10). Although they are quite distinct in style and mood, the two pictures are of a basically similar type. Both are more or less fanciful with the figure shown half-length and placed directly behind the picture plane. Both exploit the decorative effect of the pose and the plumed hat. Yet Rembrandt's '*Officer*' is more subdued in colour and lighting, his character is more sharply delineated, and the brushwork exemplifies the meticulous technique of the artist's finished pictures of the period. Pictorially speaking, it was only a short step from this to the commissioned portraits Rembrandt was to begin painting a year or two later in Amsterdam.

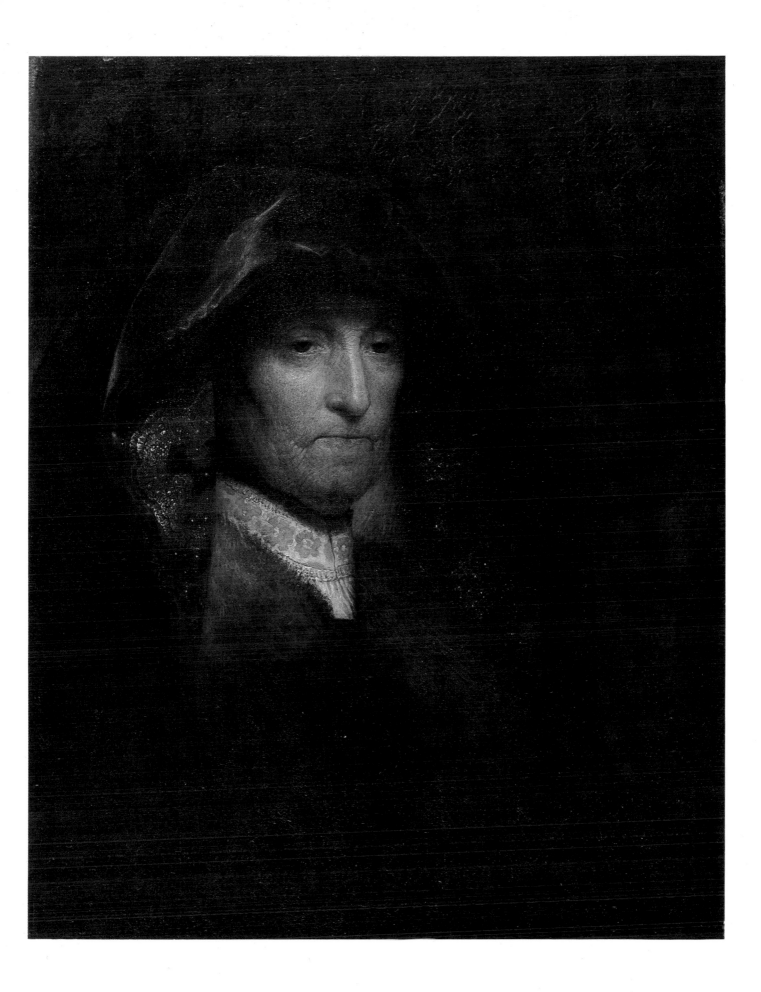

An Officer (?)

PANEL, 65 × 51 CM. SIGNED 'REMBRANDT F'. C.1630. PRIVATE COLLECTION

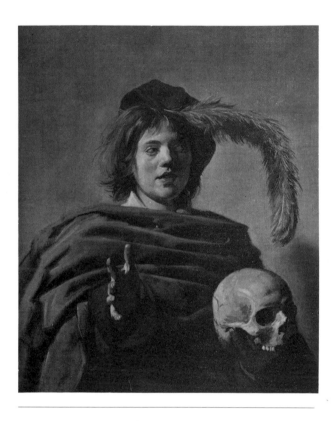

Fig. 10
FRANS HALS
A Young Man Holding a Skull

CANVAS, 92.2 × 80.8 CM. 1626–8. LONDON, NATIONAL GALLERY

This elderly, but not old, man with a large hooked nose, beady eyes and short beard is another figure who occurs several times in Rembrandt's early paintings and etchings. Like the old woman depicted in Plate 5, he has been identified with a relative of the artist: in this case, Rembrandt's father, who died in 1630. However, the justification on this occasion is even less, as the same man appears in a painting (Br. 82) and etching (M. 46) dated 1631. As with the old woman, not only his clothes but also his features vary slightly from picture to picture, revealing Rembrandt's ability to create something fresh with each new work. In some examples, the man wears a rather shabby fur garment and cap, but more often he is shown, as here, with a steel gorget round his throat and a feathered hat. Other accoutrements he sports in one painting or another are ear-rings and a gold chain with a pendant. If the gorget is intended to identify him as an army officer, he is a fierce, hard-bitten type, very different from the elegant cavaliers habitually painted by Frans Hals. One can imagine him as a soldier actually returned from the wars rather than a civilian dressed up in uniform for a social occasion.

Comparison may be made with Hals's *Young Man Holding a Skull* (Fig. 10). Although they are quite distinct in style and mood, the two pictures are of a basically similar type. Both are more or less fanciful with the figure shown half-length and placed directly behind the picture plane. Both exploit the decorative effect of the pose and the plumed hat. Yet Rembrandt's '*Officer*' is more subdued in colour and lighting, his character is more sharply delineated, and the brushwork exemplifies the meticulous technique of the artist's finished pictures of the period. Pictorially speaking, it was only a short step from this to the commissioned portraits Rembrandt was to begin painting a year or two later in Amsterdam.

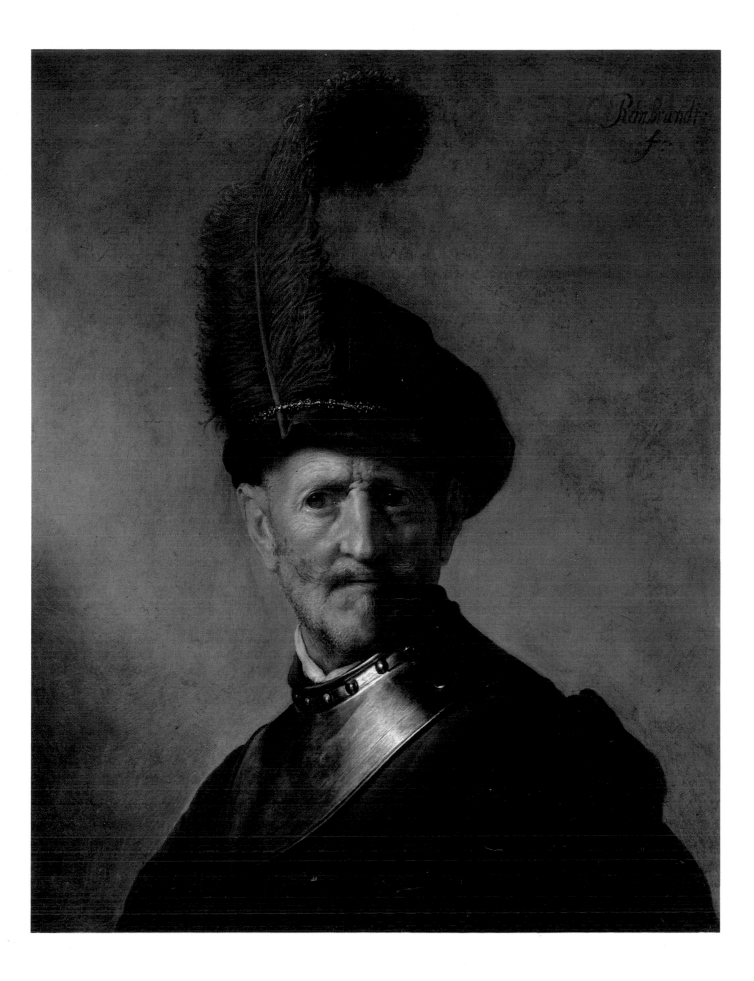

7

The Presentation of Jesus in the Temple

PANEL, 61 × 48 CM. SIGNED 'RHL 1631'. THE HAGUE, MAURITSHUIS

The story is told in St Luke's Gospel, Chapter II, vv. 22–38. In accordance with Jewish law, Mary and Joseph bring the infant Jesus into the temple at Jerusalem to be presented to the Lord. While there, they meet Simeon, an old, devout man who had been promised that he would not die until he had seen Christ. He takes the child in his arms and speaks the words later known in the services of the Church as the *Nunc Dimittis:*

Lord, now lettest thou thy servant depart in peace, according to thy word:
For mine eyes have seen thy salvation,
Which thou hast prepared before the face of all people;
A light to lighten the Gentiles, and the glory of thy people Israel.

A feature of Rembrandt's work at this period (the early 1630s) is a liking for elongated figures, diagonal compositional lines and mysterious, cavernous spaces. A little while before, he had depicted *The Presentation of Jesus in the Temple* in another painting (now in Hamburg; Br. 535) and an etching (M. 191), in both of which he had treated the subject more like a *genre* scene; the figures were more animated, Anna faced the spectator, and the space was shallower. Here, on the other hand, there is a sense of grandeur,

the mood is immensely solemn and the execution is particularly refined. This is a 'still' moment in Rembrandt's development preceding the surge of baroque turbulence which occurred in his work a few years later. A useful insight into his conception of form at this stage can be gained from the drawing of *The Angel Appearing to Manoah and his Wife* (Fig. 11). He draws the figure with long, looping lines, hardly lifting the pen from the paper, which gives an extra fluency to the forms and serves to emphasize the psychological relationship between the figures.

It is very possible that this painting is to be identified with one depicting 'Simeon in the temple holding Christ in his arms, by Rembrandt or Jan Lievens', listed in an inventory, dated 1632, of the collections of the Stadholder, Frederick-Henry (see A.B. De Vries and Others, *Rembrandt in the Mauritshuis*, 1978, p. 77). The fact that the compiler of the inventory was unable to distinguish between the work of Rembrandt and that of Lievens, with whom he shared a studio in Leyden, was not untypical; nor is it surprising since the styles of the two artists from about 1629 to 1631 were very similar. If the painting now in the Mauritshuis is the one mentioned in the inventory it would account for its richness of colour and refinement of execution, since these qualities appealed particularly to court circles at the Hague. The picture, like the famous *Passion* series now in Munich, would have left the Stadholder's collection sometime later in the seventeenth century. It was bought back by the Stadholder William IV in 1733. Shortly after this, a semi-circular top was added to the panel (now concealed under the frame).

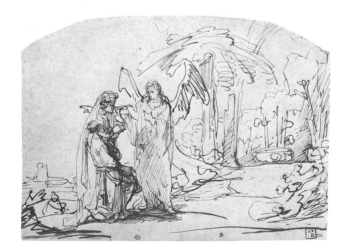

Fig. 11 (left)
The Angel Appearing to Manoah and his Wife

PEN AND BROWN INK, 18 × 25.5 CM. C.1632. ROTTERDAM, MUSEUM BOYMANS-VAN BEUNINGEN

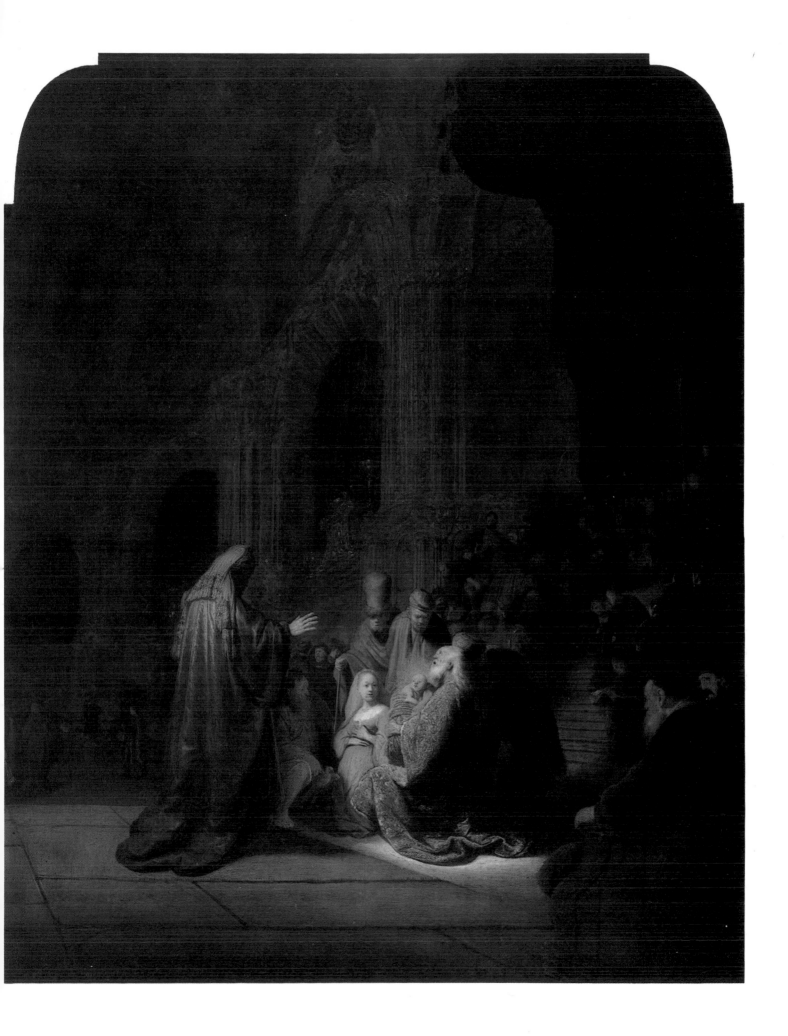

8

The Anatomy Lesson of Doctor Tulp

CANVAS, 169.5 × 216.5 CM. SIGNED 'REMBRANDT FT: 1632'. THE HAGUE, MAURITSHUIS

This picture seems to be first definitely recorded as in the Guild-Room of the Amsterdam Surgeons' Hall, which was in the St Antonies Poort, in 1693, but eighteenth-century sources state, probably reliably, that it had been there since it was painted in 1632. Contrary to some later authorities, it was never in the Anatomy Theatre, which was housed in a different building. King William I of The Netherlands bought the painting for the Mauritshuis for 32,000 guilders in 1828.

The Anatomy Lesson of Doctor Tulp was Rembrandt's first large painting and was the work with which he established his reputation on moving from Leyden to Amsterdam in the winter of 1631–2. As Riegl first pointed out in his classic study, *Das holländische Gruppenporträt*, 1931, it marked a turning-point both in Rembrandt's stylistic development and in the evolution of the Dutch corporation, or guild, portrait. For the first time the figures were unified not merely by token gestures and glances but by their common interest in an event taking place within the composition. Group portraits of surgeons' guilds, usually with a skeleton, had been a recognized category of painting in both the Northern and Southern Netherlands since the beginning of the century. The surgical dissection of corpses had also been made into established, though not frequent, official occasions, with fixed procedures rigidly controlled by the guilds. It was forbidden to hold a dissection, either in public or private, without the guild's permission, and the corpse had to be that of an executed criminal. The only dissection known to have taken place in Amsterdam in 1632 was on 31 January, when the criminal was Adriaen Adriaensz. Dr Nicolaes Pietersz. Tulp (1593–1674) was chief anatomist and *praelector* ('senior reader') of the Surgeons' Guild of Amsterdam from 1629 to 1653; he was a follower of the sixteenth-century Dutch anatomist, Vesalius, and of the Englishman, William Harvey; after his retirement he became burgomaster of Amsterdam and curator of the new university.

As W. S. Heckscher has shown (*Rembrandt's Anatomy of Dr Nicolaes Tulp*, 1958), the painting was privately commissioned by Tulp and the others portrayed in it, not collectively commissioned by the guild (as was usual), as only two of the figures, besides Tulp, were as yet officers of the guild; the names of the sitters are on the paper held by one of them. Moreover, the painting evidently alludes to a private, not a public, dissection. C.E. Kellet has argued in his important review of Heckscher's book (*Burlington Magazine*, CI, 1959, pp. 150–2) that it was at these private dissections, which were allowed prior to or following the public ones, that scientific knowledge was chiefly advanced. Public dissections, by contrast, had developed by this time into occasions for elaborate ceremonial and further symbolic 'punishment' of the criminal. They regularly began with the opening of the stomach (cf. *The Anatomy Lesson of Doctor Joan Deyman*, Plate 36), not the arm. According to Kellet, 'Dr Tulp is shown demonstrating to a few of his friends a classical dissection and comparing his findings with the magnificent new copperplates by Casserius which adorn the *Anatomy* of his countryman, Adriaen van der Spieghel, published in Venice in 1627.' It is presumably this book which is open at the plate showing the muscles and tendons of the forearm and hand. (The paper with the sitters' names on it also originally carried an anatomical engraving, now illegible, and the names may, in fact, be a later addition.)

Even so, it is not easy to see the painting as an exact illustration of a particular event. Apart from the contrivance of the grouping, the dissected arm may have been painted from an engraving rather than from the actual corpse, and it is not necessarily true that all seven onlookers would have been present on the occasion. (It has been suggested that two of them – the man holding the paper and the one on the extreme left – are additions to the composition, the second probably not by Rembrandt himself.) Essentially, the picture is to be regarded as a symbolic rather than a documentary reconstruction of one of Dr Tulp's anatomical demonstrations, perhaps the one in which he took most pride or for which he was most famous. The persons portrayed would have been admirers of his who helped pay for the picture, while the form of the composition would have been determined chiefly by pictorial considerations.

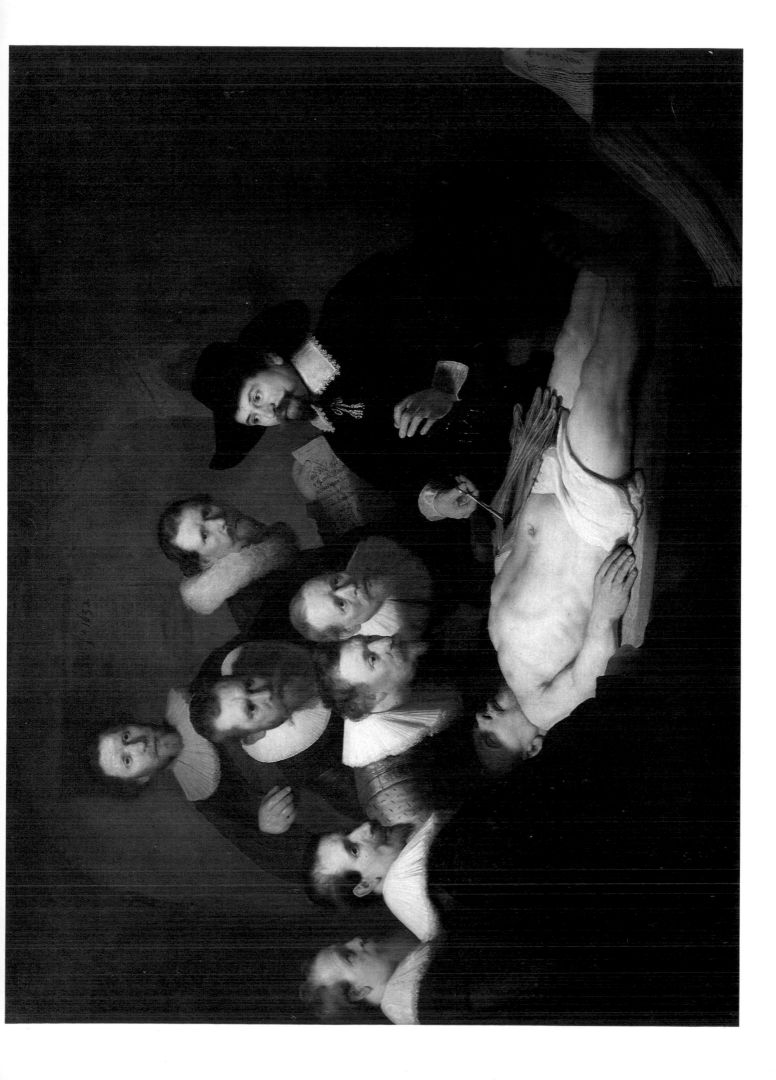

9

Saskia as Flora

CANVAS, 125 × 101 CM. SIGNED 'REMBRANDT F. 1634'. LENINGRAD, THE HERMITAGE

Besides this picture, Rembrandt represented Saskia as Flora, the classical goddess of Spring, on at least one other occasion, namely in the painting now belonging to the National Gallery, London (Fig. 12). In that instance the identification with Flora has been questioned. Lord Clark suggested Proserpina (National Art-Collections Fund Annual Report, 1939, p. 21), and Neil MacLaren (*National Gallery Catalogues: The Dutch School*, 1960, p. 334) has proposed that 'here Rembrandt was merely essaying the current Arcadian fashion'. That Rembrandt was influenced by contemporary Dutch pastoral painting as practised in Utrecht is beyond doubt, but the theme of both the Hermitage and the National Gallery pictures is surely one of 'flowers'. Moreover, the proffering of flowers with the hand in the National Gallery painting and the holding out of a single flower in pathetic irony by the sick Saskia in the portrait of her a year before her death (Dresden; Br. 108) recall the gesture of the well-known classical statue of Flora in the Farnese Collection, then in Rome. Rembrandt used the same gesture in a much later painting now in the Metropolitan Museum, New York (*c*.1657; Br. 114), perhaps using Hendrijke Stoffels as the model.

What is not in question is the degree to which both the Hermitage and National Gallery pictures illustrate Rembrandt's delight at this period of his life in exotic dress materials. In both paintings, Saskia is shown wearing the richest of fine clothes. At least some of these clothes probably came from the Near or Far East, imported by Dutch or foreign traders. His painting of the light on the dress in the Hermitage picture is especially brilliant. On the shoulder, the thickness of the paint echoes the thickness of the brocade. On the sleeve, the paint brings out the lustre in the material. Throughout, the modelling of the form in light and shade is expressive of the material's weight.

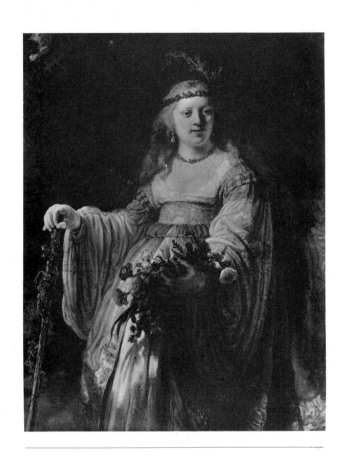

Fig. 12
Saskia as Flora

CANVAS, 123.5 × 97.5 CM. SIGNED (FALSELY?) 'REM... A 1635'. LONDON, NATIONAL GALLERY

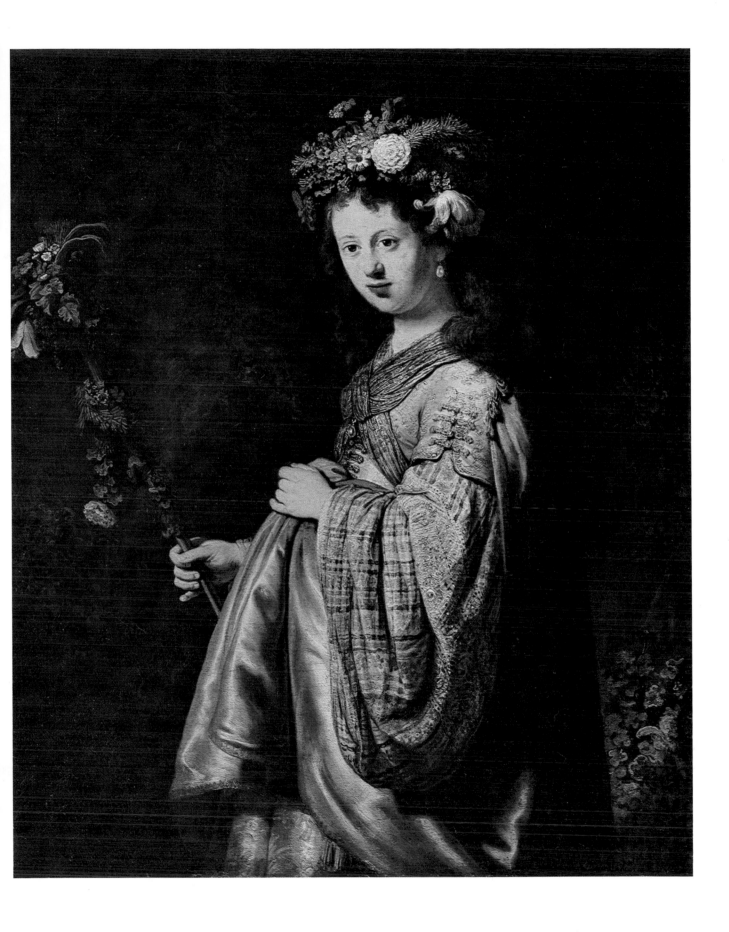

10

A Young Woman in Fancy Dress

PANEL, 98 × 70 CM. SIGNED 'REMBRANDT F. 1635 (?)'. PRIVATE COLLECTION

The date of this picture has also been read as 1638 but, as H. Gerson has pointed out (*Rembrandt* by A. Bredius, revised by H. Gerson, 1969, p. 556 under No. 104), 1635 is more likely since in the following year the artist's pupil, Govaert Flinck, based his portraits of a shepherd and shepherdess on precisely this type of Rembrandt. Moreover, the lighting and costume of the figure bear some resemblance to the woman on the extreme left of *Belshazzar's Feast* (Plate 11), which may be dated about 1635.

The young woman in the present painting has sometimes been identified as the artist's wife, Saskia, but this is surely wrong, since the face is longer and conventionally prettier than hers. That Rembrandt could, however, endow Saskia with great charm, if not beauty, is shown by the portrait drawing he made of her a few days after their engagement to be married (Fig. 13). Rembrandt's Dutch inscription on this reads in translation: 'This is a drawing of my wife, made when she was 21 years old, the third day after our betrothal – the 8th of June 1633.' The use of silver-point shows how private this portrait was intended to be, for silver-point is an exceptionally fine and delicate medium, and so faint that a drawing executed in it can only be appreciated at close range. In the light of the discussion of *Saskia as Flora* (see note to Plate 9), it may be observed that the figure holds a single flower in her hand. In conception and to some extent in style, there is a parallel between this drawing and Rubens's portraits of his young second wife, Hélène Fourment.

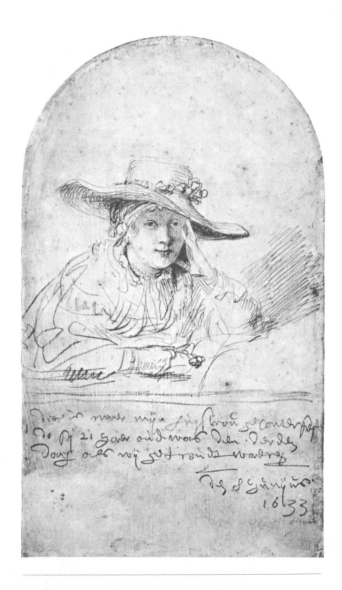

Fig. 13
Saskia in a Straw Hat

SILVER-POINT ON WHITE PREPARED VELLUM, 18.5 × 10.7 CM.
INSCRIBED BY THE ARTIST AND DATED, 1633. WEST BERLIN,
KUPFERSTICHKABINETT

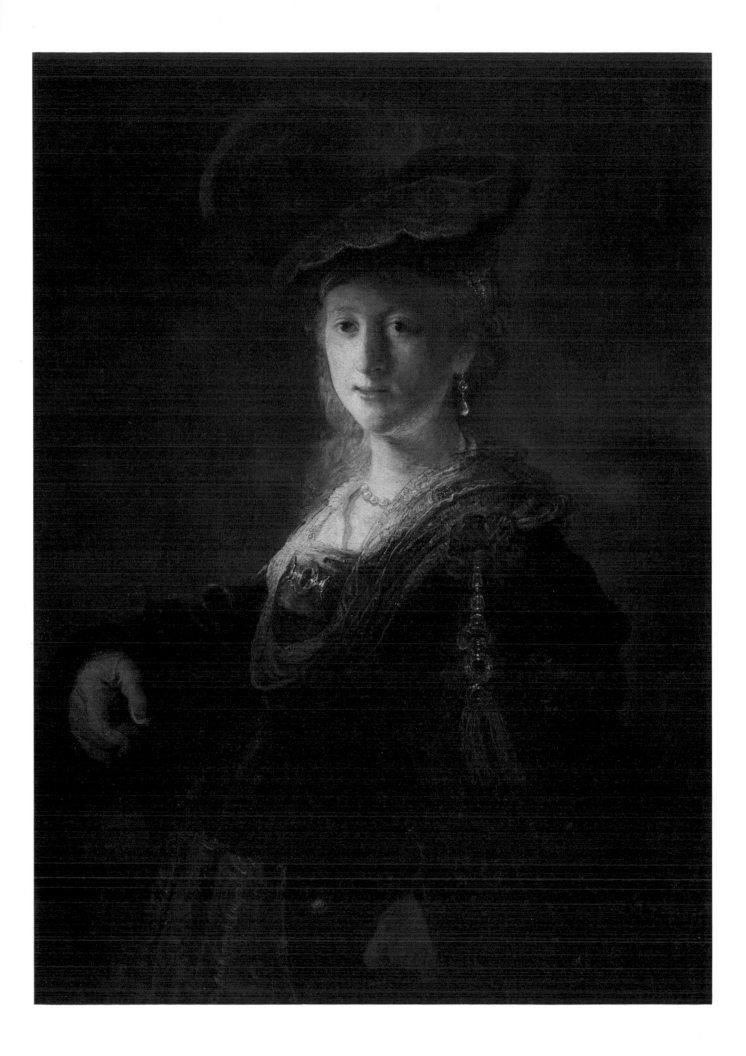

11

Belshazzar's Feast: The Writing on the Wall

CANVAS, 167 × 209.5 CM. SIGNED 'REMBRANDT F. 163.' LONDON, NATIONAL GALLERY

The subject is taken from the Book of Daniel, Chapter V. Belshazzar, feasting with a thousand of his lords, wives and concubines, commands the gold and silver vessels, which his father had looted from the temple at Jerusalem, to be brought in and filled with wine. At this, a mysterious hand appears and writes on the wall: MENE, MENE, TEKEL, UPHARSIN. Belshazzar, terrified, sends for soothsayers to decipher the writing but they all fail, and eventually the Jew, Daniel, is summoned. He explains that the words mean that, because of his sacrilege, Belshazzar's days are numbered and his kingdom will fall. That very night, Belshazzar is slain.

Rembrandt, contrary to western pictorial tradition, depicts the words vertically downwards, beginning at the top right, and follow a form found in Jewish, not Christian, literature. Specifically, they are very close to the version printed in *De termino vitae* by the Jewish author, Menasseh ben Israel, published in Amsterdam in 1639, and this has led some critics to suppose that the

picture must have been painted in or after that year. However, it is now generally agreed that this is too late on stylistic grounds, and a date of around 1635 is favoured. It is pointed out that Rembrandt etched Menasseh ben Israel's portrait in 1636 (M. 56) and so could have had access to his manuscript in advance of publication or to his research. The resemblance in the lettering is too close for coincidence.

The composition is vaguely reminiscent of a painting by Lastman of *The Fury of Ahasuerus*, now in Warsaw, as was first observed by Keith Roberts (*Connoisseur Year Book*, 1965, pp. 65–70), and Rembrandt may also have had in mind Lievens's early *Feast of Esther*, in Raleigh, North Carolina. The figure at the lower right bending back and presenting the top of her head to the spectator is perhaps the first sign of Venetian influence in Rembrandt's art. But whatever the precedents, this is a spectacular example of Rembrandt's own baroque style at its most vigorous. The powerful figure of Belshazzar constitutes a tilting axis, either side of which subsidiary figures cower in fear.

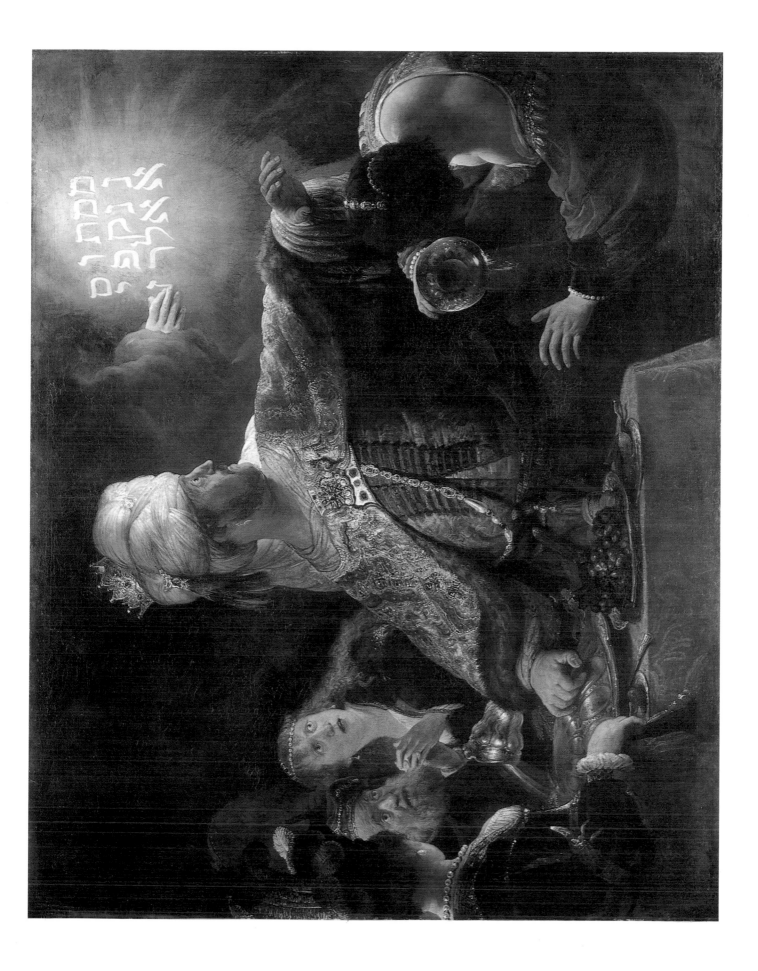

12

Uzziah Stricken with Leprosy

PANEL, 101 × 79 CM. SIGNED 'REMBRANDT F. 1635'. CHATSWORTH (DERBYSHIRE)

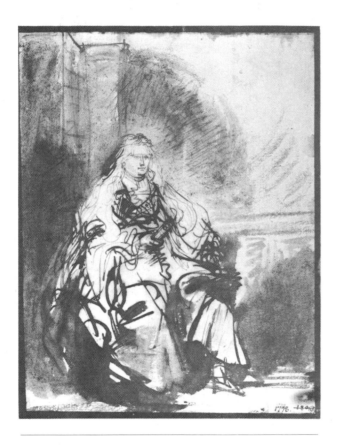

Fig. 14
Study for the Etching, 'The Great Jewish Bride'

PEN AND BROWN WASH, 24.1 × 19.3 CM. C.1635. STOCKHOLM,
NATIONALMUSEUM

'Uzziah stricken with leprosy' (2 Chronicles, Chapter XXVI, vv.18–19) has most recently been suggested as the subject of this painting. The story is also told, and in greater detail, by Flavius Josephus in his *Jewish Antiquities*, Book IX, paragraph 222, and it is likely that Rembrandt used that as his source. King Uzziah was banished from the temple and struck down with leprosy for presuming to burn incense at the altar, a privilege reserved for the priests. The problem in the case of this painting – not uncharacteristic, as we have seen elsewhere – is that Rembrandt includes no specific symbol or object on which the identification of the subject might depend. Yet, in contrast to most unidentified single figures in his *œuvre*, the expression is not one of contemplation or repose. On the contrary, the face is tense with rage or fear, which would fit Uzziah or some other Old Testament character.

In type, the figure is similar to a number of others dating from the mid-1630s, among which Belshazzar in *Belshazzar's Feast* (Plate 11) is conspicuous; further examples occur among the etchings. The characteristics of this type are a massive square head and body, a thick beard, a broad cap or turban and very heavy clothes. There is a hint of the Near East or of Jewry about the figure, though it is hard to say exactly why. The study reproduced here (Fig. 14) for the etching, *The Great Jewish Bride* (M. 90 – though there is no good reason to think that she is Jewish), shows the female equivalent of this figure. As with the *Old Woman Wearing a Black Head-Scarf* and the '*Officer*' (Plates 5 and 6), the artist's rendering varies each time the same model is used, and there is no clear distinction between a religious and a non-religious subject. The stylistic approach throughout is strongly baroque, that is, the forms are very fully, not to say aggressively, modelled and the face is richly animated.

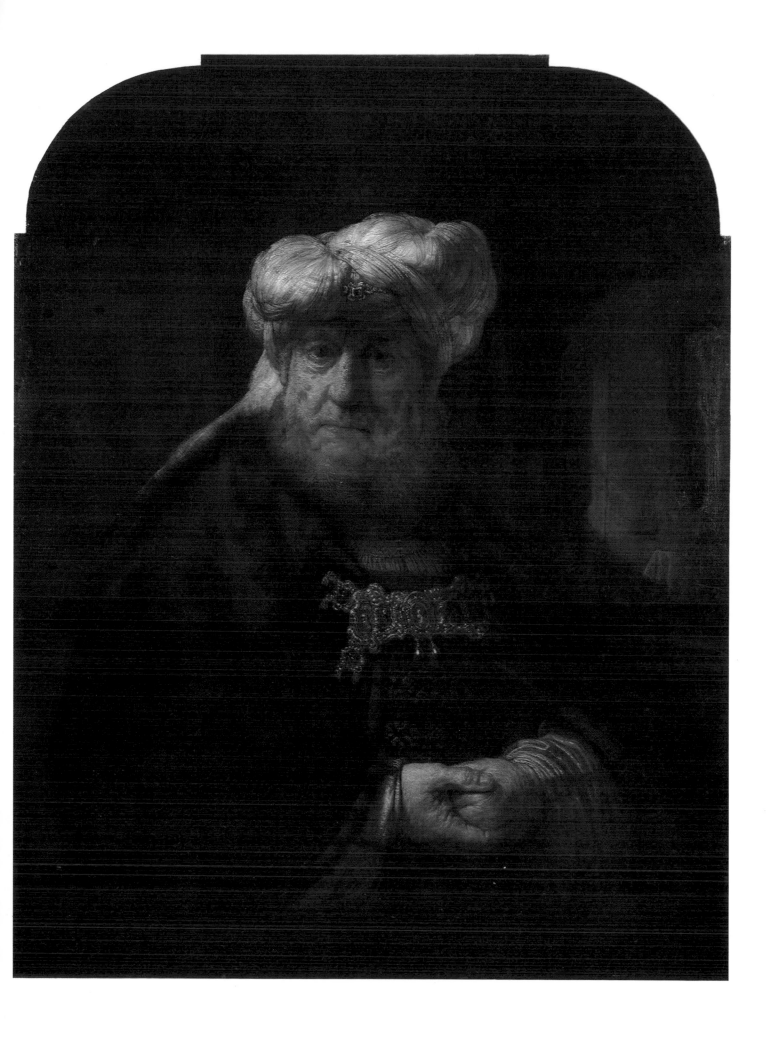

13

The Entombment of Christ

PANEL, 32 × 40.5 CM. C.1639. UNIVERSITY OF GLASGOW, HUNTERIAN ART GALLERY

This monochrome sketch in oils is fairly closely related to the painting of the same subject (Fig. 15) which Rembrandt completed in 1639 as part of a series on the Passion of Christ for the Stadholder, Prince Frederick-Henry of Orange (1584–1647). This series, which is now in Munich, comprises five paintings and may originally have included a sixth, *Christ on the Cross* (Le Mas d'Agenais, France; Br. 543A), executed first, in 1631, which for some reason never entered the Stadholder's collection, though he was certainly aware of Rembrandt's work by this date (see note to Plate 5). It is possible that Rembrandt painted the first picture or pictures on his own initiative, persuading Frederick-Henry to buy them through his Secretary, Constantin Huygens (1596–1687), and that a commission only resulted later. *The Raising of the Cross* and *The Descent from the Cross* were evidently completed by 1633. Between 1636 and 1639, Rembrandt wrote seven letters to Huygens, which are mostly about this series, although little is said in them about art. They are the only letters by Rembrandt known (see H. Gerson, *Seven Letters by Rembrandt*, 1961). In the first letter (probably of February 1636), Rembrandt explains that the *Ascension* is complete (it is dated that year) and that the *Resurrection* and *Entombment* are 'more than half done'. In the third letter, dated 12 January 1639, he writes that 'through studious application' these two paintings are now finished and that in them he has expressed 'the greatest and most natural movement' (*die meeste ende die naetureelste beweechgelickheyt* – for a discussion of this phrase and its significance see Introductory text). In a further letter, accompanying the two pictures when they were despatched, Rembrandt considered that they were worth 1,000 guilders each but he later (13 February 1639) reduced his price to 600 guilders each, not including 44 guilders for the two ebony frames. The large sums Rembrandt asked and in part received are reflected in the very high quality of the execution of the five paintings. Though less minutely detailed than his earliest works, they are finished with

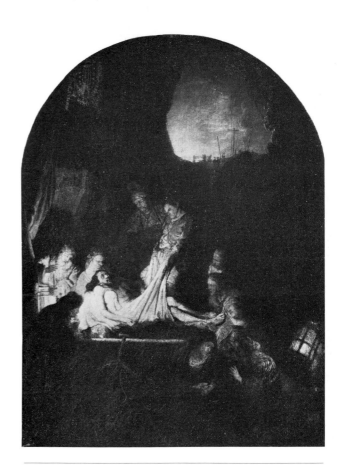

Fig. 15
The Entombment of Christ

CANVAS, 92.5 × 70 CM. 1636–9. MUNICH, ALTE PINAKOTHEK

the utmost conscientiousness and skill. Both the lights and darks glow and the forms are very precisely defined.

The question is, whether the Glasgow sketch was a study for the central group in the *Entombment* or whether it was a by-product. The first hypothesis

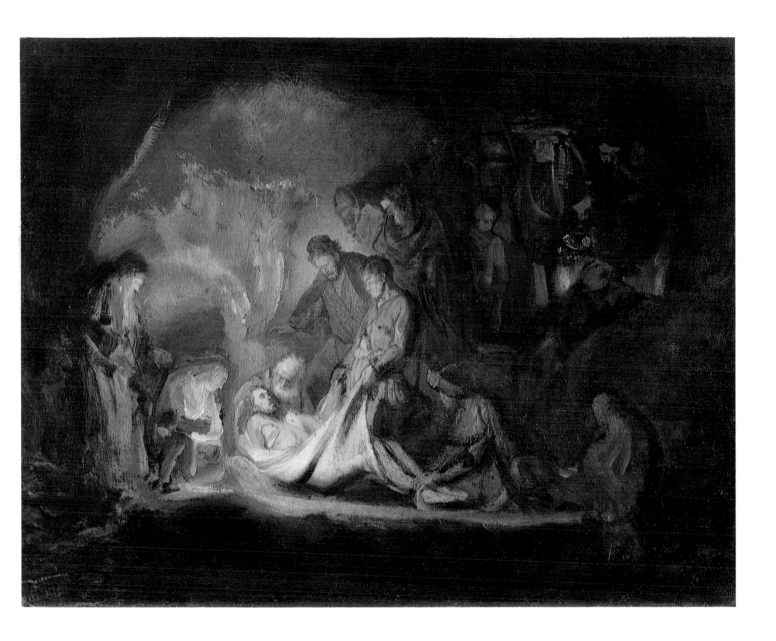

would be stronger if Rembrandt's statement that the Munich painting was 'more than half done' in February 1636 was an untruth and if the painting (and therefore the sketch) had been begun as well as finished in 1639, for the style of the sketch would be easier to reconcile with the later rather than the earlier date. During the last half of the 1630s, Rembrandt's style was still changing rapidly, and the trend towards calmness and introspection which is evident here only revealed itself clearly at the very end of the decade (though it might, admittedly, have emerged sooner in a sketch than in a finished picture). The

alternative to considering the Glasgow painting as a study for the Munich picture is to regard it as a study for an etching (never executed), and some scholars have argued in favour of this irrespective of the date. Unlike many seventeenth-century artists, Rembrandt did not habitually make oil sketches for his finished paintings, but did so on several occasions for his etchings, and the Glasgow sketch may well be an example.

It may be identical with No. 111 in Rembrandt's inventory of 1656: 'One sketch of the Entombment of Christ by Rembrandt.'

14

The Risen Christ Appearing to the Magdalene ('Noli Me Tangere')

PANEL, 61 × 49.5 CM. SIGNED 'REMBRANDT F. 1638'. LONDON, BUCKINGHAM PALACE (REPRODUCED BY GRACIOUS PERMISSION OF HER MAJESTY THE QUEEN)

The subject is taken from St John's Gospel, Chapter XX, vv. 11–17. Christ carries a spade and wears a broad straw hat, the traditional allusion in art to the Magdalene's mistaking him for the gardener. The landscape (detail, Fig. 16) is particularly fresh and beautiful. On the back of the panel is a transcript of a poem in Dutch by Rembrandt's friend, Jeremias de Dekker (1609/10–1666); this was first published in 1660 in *De Hollantsche Parnas*, a poetry anthology which contained several references to Rembrandt:

As I read the story told to us by Saint John
And there beside it see the picture, then I think:
When has the pen ever been so faithfully imitated by the
    brush

Or dead paint been so nearly brought to life?
Christ seems to say: Mary, be not afraid,
It is I, and death no longer has any part in thy Lord:
She, as yet only half believing this,
Seems to hover between joy and sorrow, hope and fear.
The rock of the grave rises by art high into the air
And, rich with shadows, gives a majesty
To the whole work. Your masterly strokes,
Friend Rembrandt, have I seen first pass over the panel,
Therefore shall my pen write a poem to your gifted brush
And my ink speak the fame of your paint.

In the heading to the poem, de Dekker states that he had seen Rembrandt at work on the picture and that it was painted for the Amsterdam clerk and visitor of the sick, H.F. Waterloos.

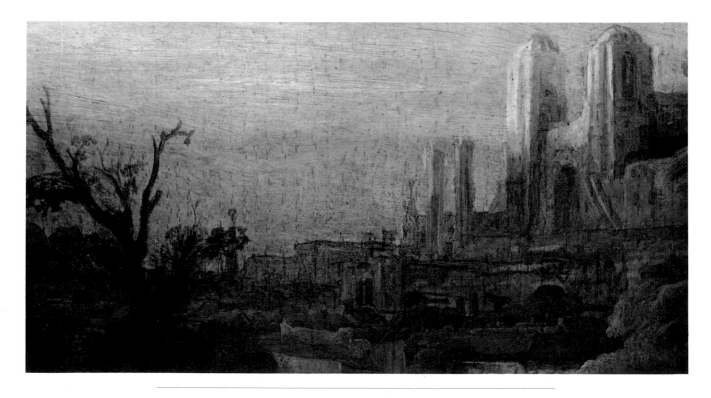

Fig. 16
Detail from 'The Risen Christ Appearing to the Magdalene' ('Noli Me Tangere')

SEE PLATE 14

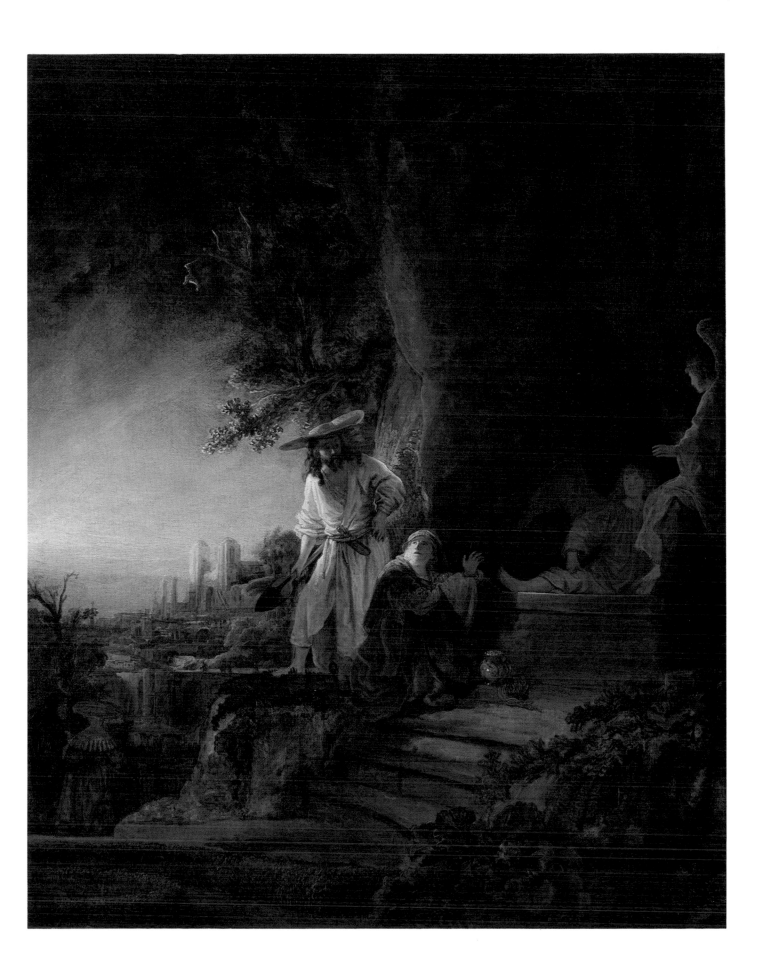

15

Self-Portrait

PANEL, 62.5 × 50 CM. SIGNED 'REMBRANDT F. 163.'. LOS ANGELES, THE NORTON SIMON MUSEUM OF ART

Although Rembrandt's habitual method of presenting himself in his self-portraits was as a formidable working artist and social misfit, there were occasions, especially during the first half of his career, when he appeared as a man anxious to conform. In those portraits in which this is the case, he is seen as elegantly dressed, with his hair neatly brushed, his moustache and beard trimmed, and with the lighting in the picture so arranged as to make his features seem more regular and his skin smoother than they probably were in reality. What is more, the handling of the paint is carried to a higher degree of finish than usual, recalling the brushwork used in his commissioned portraits.

The Norton Simon *Self-Portrait* is a notable example of this type. It probably dates from 1639, the year in which Rembrandt moved into his grand house in the Jodenbreestraat; if so, this might account for his choice of pictorial approach here. At about the same time, Rembrandt's style generally became more restrained and introspective. One sign of this is that he began studying Italian Renaissance art, the influence of which is evident in a classical poise which characterizes some of his paintings, including the present one, during these years. His sources were chiefly copies and engravings, but in 1639 he saw and sketched Raphael's famous *Portrait of Baldassare Castiglione* (now in the Louvre) when it was put up for sale in Amsterdam by the dealer, Lucas van Uffelen. His sketch (Fig. 17), which is a free rather than accurate copy of the painting, bears an inscription which reads in translation: 'The Count Balthasar Castiglione by Raphael / sold for 3500 guilders / the whole collection of Lucas van Nuffeelen fetched / fl. 59456. Anno 1639.' In the same year, Rembrandt made a *Self-Portrait* etching (M. 24) based on this drawing, and in 1640 he executed the well-known painted *Self-Portrait* (Br. 34) in the National Gallery, London, reversing the composition and varying it yet again. It is not suggested that the Norton Simon *Self-Portrait* was also based on this picture by Raphael, which Rembrandt may still not have seen, but it does recall a familiar Italian Renaissance portrait type. The composition is in the form of a stable pyramid, with the head turned towards the spectator and the shoulders and upper part of the body shown in three-quarter view.

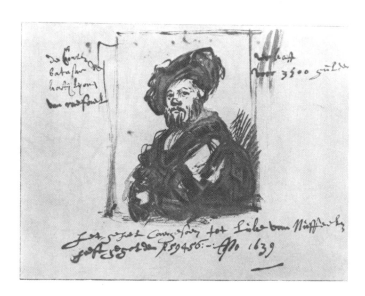

Fig. 17
Portrait of Baldassare Castiglione, after Raphael

PEN AND BROWN WASH, 16.3 × 20.7 CM. SIGNED, INSCRIBED AND
DATED, 1639. VIENNA, ALBERTINA

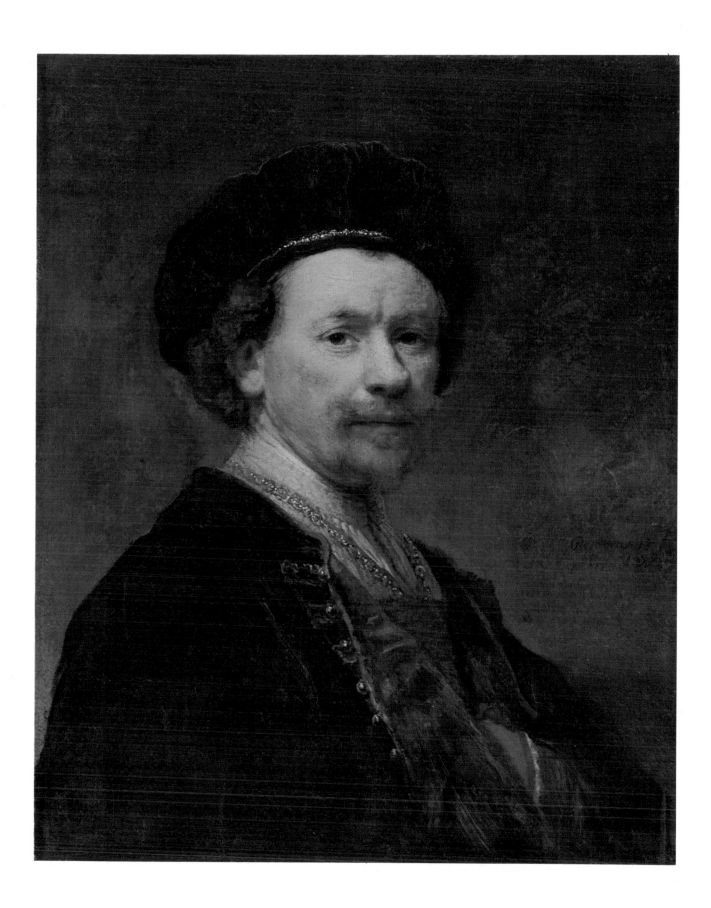

16

Portrait of Agatha Bas

CANVAS, 104.5 × 85 CM. SIGNED 'REMBRANDT F. 1641'. LONDON, BUCKINGHAM PALACE (REPRODUCED BY GRACIOUS PERMISSION OF HER MAJESTY THE QUEEN)

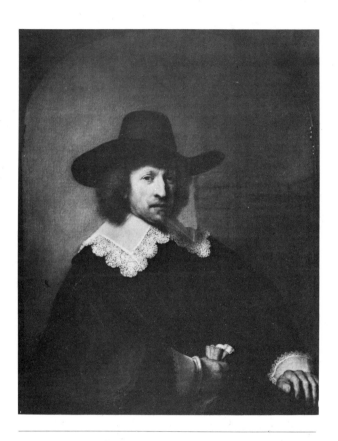

Fig. 18
Portrait of Nicolaes van Bambeeck, Husband of Agatha Bas

CANVAS, 105.5 × 84 CM. SIGNED 'REMBRANDT F. 1641'. BRUSSELS, MUSÉE ROYAL DES BEAUX-ARTS (COPYRIGHT A.C.L. BRUSSELS)

The companion portrait of the sitter's husband (Fig. 18; Br. 218), also dated 1641, is in the Musée Royal des Beaux-Arts, Brussels; they remained together until 1809. The identification of the sitters as the wealthy Amsterdam merchant, Nicolaes van Bambeeck, and his wife, Agatha Bas, is due to I.H. van Eeghen (*Een Amsterdamse Burgemeestersdochter van Rembrandt in Buckingham Palace*, 1958). They were typical members of the high merchant and diplomatic class which sat to Rembrandt in fairly large numbers in the 1630s and early 1640s. However, by this stage the artist's approach was becoming more personal and his interpretation more penetrating than in the previous decade (though the wife's portrait is more remarkable from these points of view than that of the husband). In fact, both portraits belong to a phase (which includes *The Night Watch*) during which Rembrandt seems to have been more than usually interested in illusiontistic effects. The figures are placed in painted openings, which give the impression of being windows, though in form they are closer to picture frames. Part of the hand in each case overlaps this frame, as does the woman's fan, which serves to create the illusion that the figures are physically present; in addition, the husband seems to lean slightly out towards the spectator. Apart from his left arm, the composition of his portrait conforms to a Renaissance pyramidal type, with the right forearm aligned with the base of the pyramid. With Agatha Bas's portrait, the interest lies not so much in the composition as in the intentness of the sitter's gaze and the brilliant painting of the white lace, the embroidered bodice and the fan.

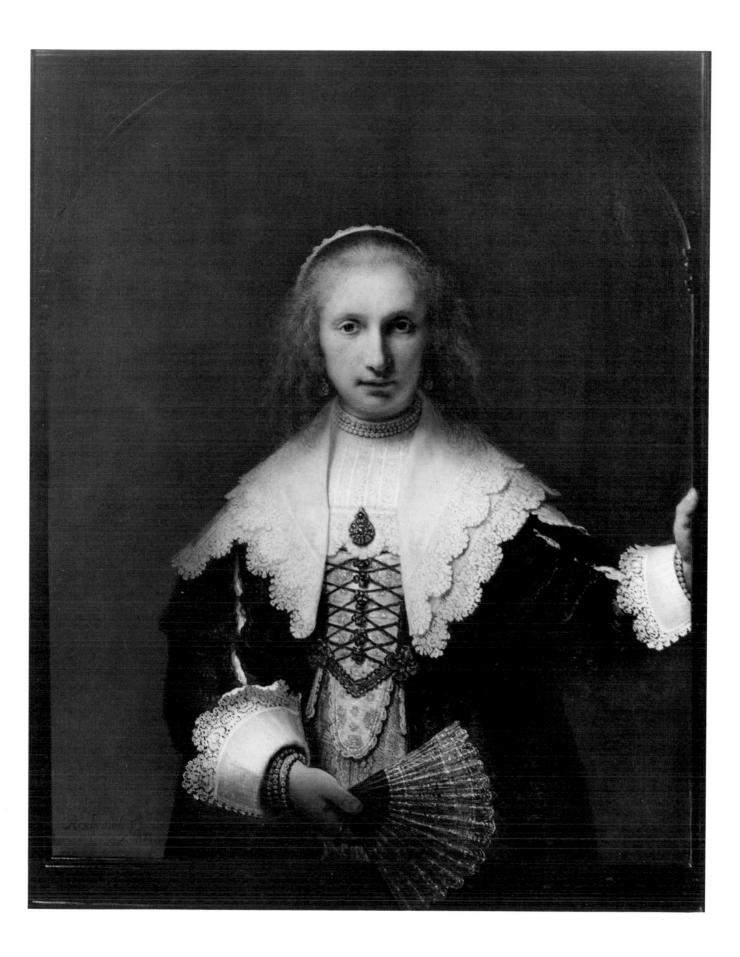

17

Landscape with a Church

PANEL, 42 × 60 CM. C.1640. PRIVATE COLLECTION

A Northern Gothic church and a Dutch drawbridge are the central features of this composition but they are situated in a small ancient town of seemingly Turkish character and in a remote, ghostly landscape. Rembrandt appears to conjure up here a sort of Near Eastern antiquity belonging to no specific time or place, made all the more romantic and mysterious by the western travellers who approach the city. The picture, if it is by Rembrandt (which is not quite certain), was probably painted around 1640 and reflects the influence of Hercules Seghers, eight of whose painted landscapes were in Rembrandt's collection. Seghers was also a highly individual master of landscape etching (Fig. 19), and some scholars have suggested that this painting may be by him. The composition of the painting shows the general trend towards simplification and tranquillity which was characteristic of Rembrandt's style at this time. The same tendency can also be seen in the evolution of Dutch realistic landscape painting in the 1640s, as exemplified by the work of Jan van Goyen and Salomon van Ruysdael.

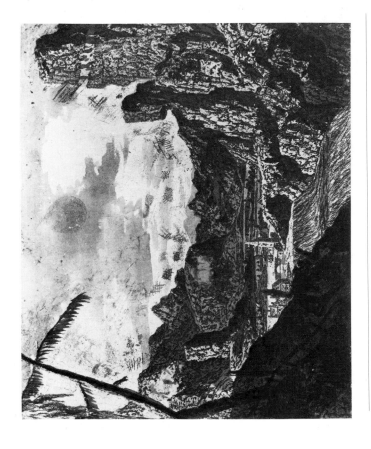

Fig. 19
HERCULES SEGHERS
River Valley with a Waterfall

ETCHING, PRINTED IN BLUE WITH AN OVERLAY OF GREY WASH, 15.6 × 18.8 CM. C.1615-25(?).
LONDON, BRITISH MUSEUM

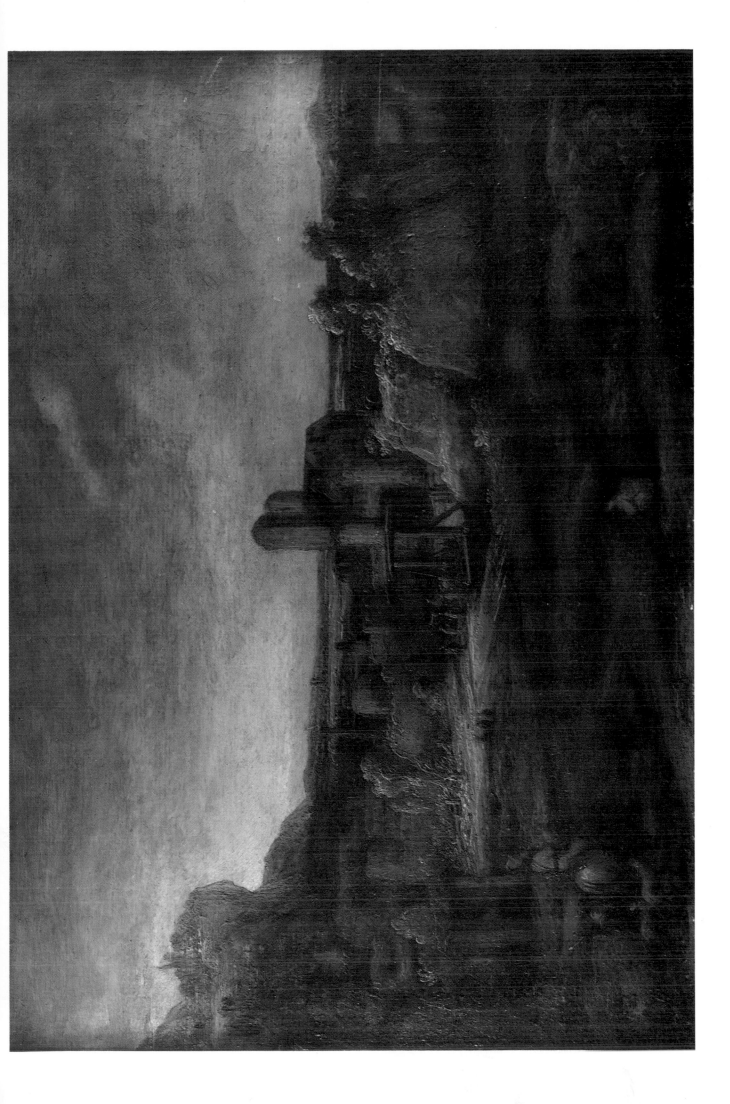

18

The Militia Company of Captain Frans Banning Cocq ('The Night Watch')

CANVAS, 359 × 438 CM. SIGNED 'REMBRANDT F. 1642'. AMSTERDAM, RIJKSMUSEUM

The painting hung in the Great Room of the Kloveniersdoelen (the Musketeers' Assembly Hall) in Amsterdam until 1715, when it was transferred to the Town Hall; it was moved to the Rijksmuseum in 1808.

The literature on this famous painting, which has been almost as much abused as praised, is immense, and no more than a few selected points can be mentioned here. As is shown by early copies (Fig. 20), the canvas has been cut, probably when it was moved to the Town Hall in 1715; some 60 cm., incorporating two background figures and a baby, have been removed from the left side, and lesser amounts from the other three sides. This unbalances the composition (the arch in the background was originally nearer the centre) and compresses the figures into too confined a space. In all, twenty-six figures are now fully or partly visible, including three children (or dwarfs?), and small parts of five more figures can just be discerned in the background. (For these and other particulars, see MacLaren, *National Gallery Catalogues: The Dutch School*, 1960, pp. 343–9). To the right of the arch there is a shield, added later, bearing the names of eighteen of the persons portrayed. According to two of them who gave evidence on Rembrandt's behalf during the investigation into his financial affairs in 1658/9, he was paid a total of 1,600 guilders; the sitters contributed an average of 100 guilders each, the sum varying with their prominence in the picture.

A reference in the family album of the captain, Frans Banning Cocq (1605–55), states that the painting shows him directing his lieutenant, Willem van Ruytenburch, to order the company to march out; the captain is in black with a red sash, the lieutenant in pale yellow carrying a ceremonial lance. At least since the cleaning of the picture in 1946/7, it has been evident that the scene takes place in daylight, with

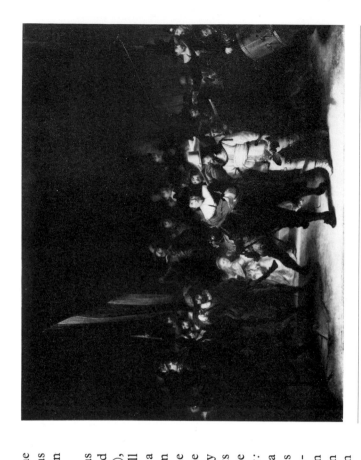

Fig. 20
UNKNOWN ARTIST
Copy of 'The Night Watch'

PANEL, 67 × 85.5 CM (APPROX.). BEFORE 1715. LONDON, NATIONAL GALLERY (ON LOAN TO THE RIJKSMUSEUM)

continued overleaf

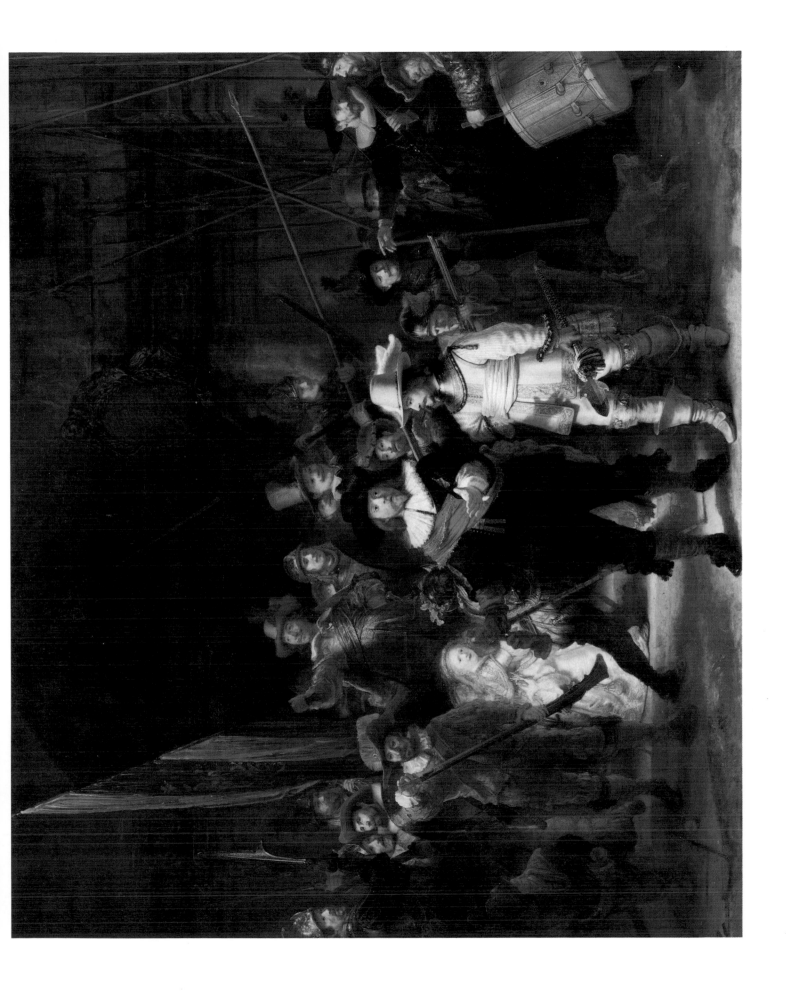

19

Detail from 'The Militia Company of Captain Frans Banning Cocq' ('The Night Watch')

SEE PLATE 18

continued

the sun streaming down from the top left. A further cleaning completed in 1980 shows that the tones are predominantly cool. The traditional title, *The Night Watch*, which dates from the late eighteenth century, is therefore erroneous but it would be absurdly pedantic to suggest changing it now. Local militia companies were raised in the sixteenth century during the Dutch war of independence to protect the cities from invasion by the Spanish armies active in Flanders, but by Rembrandt's time they were no longer needed in a military capacity except on the frontier and were kept in being for social reasons. It has been presumed that the company in Rembrandt's painting is marching out to take part in a shooting match. The girl to the left of Banning Cocq carries a dead fowl at her girdle, perhaps as a prize or trophy to be awarded to the winner of the competition; the choice of bird is no doubt a punning allusion to the Captain's name. Another suggested interpretation is that the picture represents the parade of the Amsterdam militia companies in honour of Marie des Médicis, the exiled Queen Mother of France, when she visited the Dutch capital in 1638 (see W. Martin, *Van Nachtwacht tot Feeststoet*, 1947). Apparently several companies ordered paintings to commemorate this event. A third suggestion, put forward by W. Hellinga (*Rembrandt fecit 1642*, 1956), is that *The Night Watch* is an allegory of the triumph of the city of Amsterdam inspired by Vondel's poetic drama, *Gysbrecht van Aemstel* (1638). This suggestion rests on the alleged presence of the letters 'GYSB' in the chasing of the lieutenant's armoured collar, which are, however, no more than shadowy lines forming part of the decoration. What is more, there is no reference to any allegorical significance in contemporary documents. Historical

allegories were, it is true, painted by Dutch artists in the seventeenth century and some included contemporary portraits, but, if *The Night Watch* had been a picture of this type, it is inconceivable that allegorical figures would not have been introduced as well. In a city which was about to proclaim its triumphs in a vast new Town Hall, loaded with sculptural symbolism, a *disguised* allegory would have been both unnecessary and pointless.

This is not to say that *The Night Watch* is visually just like any other group portrait. Some characters are represented much more distinctly than others, and the eighteen who subscribed are supplemented by almost as many subordinate figures, included by Rembrandt for pictorial effect. The group portrait is here transformed into an action picture: a work of dazzling inventiveness and splendour or, as some critics have maintained, a wildly over-inflated account of a very ordinary event. It marked at once a revolution in, and the swan-song of, the militia company portrait for, shortly afterwards, the demand for these portraits ceased and artists turned to the quieter, more humdrum themes of the guild portrait and the portrait of the board of hospital governors. Moreover, Rembrandt himself was never to paint such a flamboyant or such a fully baroque picture again. However, one thing is certain: *The Night Watch* was a success at the time. The story that it was disliked by those portrayed and that it was the cause of the decline in Rembrandt's contemporary reputation (which did occur to some extent in the later 1640s and 1650s) is a romantic fiction invented in the nineteenth century. Indeed, it is a wonder how this fiction arose, since there is abundant evidence to show that for more than a hundred years after it was painted *The Night Watch* was widely regarded as Rembrandt's most celebrated work.

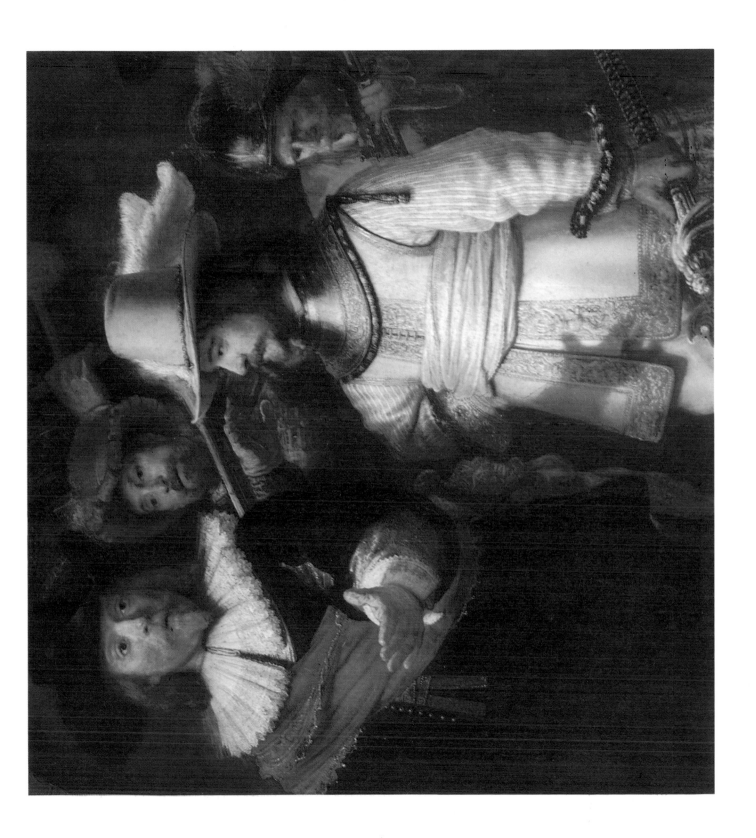

20

Christ and the Woman Taken in Adultery

PANEL WITH ROUNDED UPPER CORNERS, 83.8 × 65.4 CM. SIGNED 'REMBRANDT. F. 1644'. LONDON, NATIONAL GALLERY

The painting is probably that mentioned in the inventory, dated 1657, of the Amsterdam art dealer, Johannes des Renialme, where it is described (in Dutch) as 'A picture of the woman taken in adultery by Rembrandt van Rhyn'; it was valued at 1,500 guilders, half as much again as any other painting in his collection and only slightly less than the artist received for *The Night Watch*. *The Woman taken in Adultery* was later owned by Willem Six (nephew of Jan Six, see Plate 32), at whose sale in Amsterdam in 1734 it was bought in at 2,500 guilders. After ap-

parently remaining with the Six family until 1803, it was bought in at a London sale in 1807 at 5,000 guineas and sold the following day to J.J. Angerstein, from whom it was acquired by the National Gallery in 1824.

The subject is taken from St John's Gospel, Chapter VIII, vv. 2–11. A woman found committing adultery was brought before Jesus in the temple by the scribes and pharisees to see whether he would uphold the Mosaic law, which demanded that she be stoned to death. He replied by stooping down and writing with his finger on the ground: 'He that is without sin among you, let him cast the first stone.' One by one the woman's accusers stole away and she was pardoned.

The high price at which the picture was valued from Rembrandt's lifetime down to the early nineteenth century bears witness to its enduring popularity. It was probably always a 'collector's piece' and is the kind of relatively early, highly finished Rembrandt which appealed to the taste of the seventeenth, eighteenth and early nineteenth centuries. Indeed it looks as if the artist deliberately painted the central figure-group in an earlier, more finished style than was usual for him at this date (1644), no doubt to please the patron. The sketchier background figures are in the manner of the drawings from nature (Fig. 21) which Rembrandt had been making for the past decade. The bright colours and meticulous brushwork used for the central group are in the manner of *The Presentation of Jesus in the Temple* of 1631 (Plate 7); the composition is also reminiscent of that painting. However, the surrounding figures are handled more broadly and the receding diagonals of the earlier work have been rearranged so as to form a pattern more nearly parallel to the picture surface. The fiery golds and reds of the throne at the upper right form an area glowing with colour and touched with the mystery typical of Rembrandt's paintings in his middle period.

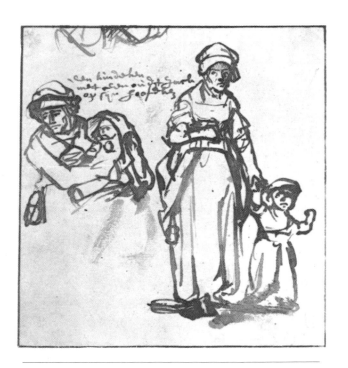

Fig. 21
Sheet of Studies of Women and Children

PEN AND INK, 13.4 × 12.8 CM. C.1636. LONDON, PRIVATE COLLECTION

21

A Young Girl Leaning on a Window-Sill

CANVAS, 81.5 × 66 CM. SIGNED 'REMBRANDT FT. 1645'. LONDON, DULWICH COLLEGE GALLERY

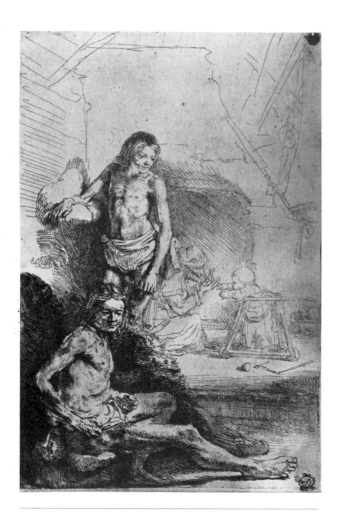

Fig. 22
Studies from the Nude, with a Woman and Baby
lightly etched in the Background

ETCHING, 19.4 × 22.8 CM. C.1646. LONDON, BRITISH MUSEUM

This painting of a young girl exhibits a freedom from tension rare in Rembrandt's work; not even his portraits of Saskia show a similar quality more than once or twice (for example, the silver-point drawing reproduced as Fig. 13). In the Dulwich picture he portrays, in a moment of ease, fresh-faced girlhood without ulterior motives. The same feeling transferred to a religious context is expressed in the paintings of the Holy Family illustrated in the next two Plates. This is Rembrandt, in mid-career, revealing himself at his most relaxed and most beguiling.

Underlying the approach here is a new objectivity in his attitude to the human figure. He does not seek to dramatize it, caricature it or make it appear in motion, but is content to represent it for its own sake. One is more conscious in this picture than usual of the existence of the studio, of the daily work of drawing and painting the posed model. The same may be said of the etching of a boy shown in Fig. 22 (it is the same boy etched twice). The figure exists simply to be represented – which is not to say that Rembrandt is interested only in pure form without emotional expression. He made a preliminary sketch of the girl in black chalk (now in the Princes Gate Collection, The Courtauld Institute; Ben. 700); in this her arms are posed differently and her hair is untidier. However, the existence of the sketch does not mean that the picture was not painted from the life. Perhaps, as in the drawing, the girl was leaning on a small table or desk, and the drawing further suggests that the studio was light, not dark (the etching indicates this even more clearly). Rembrandt would thus have added the dark background and the suggestion of a window from imagination.

The figure is as richly modelled in three dimensions as any in the artist's earlier work, but the handling is now broader and the treatment as a whole more atmospheric.

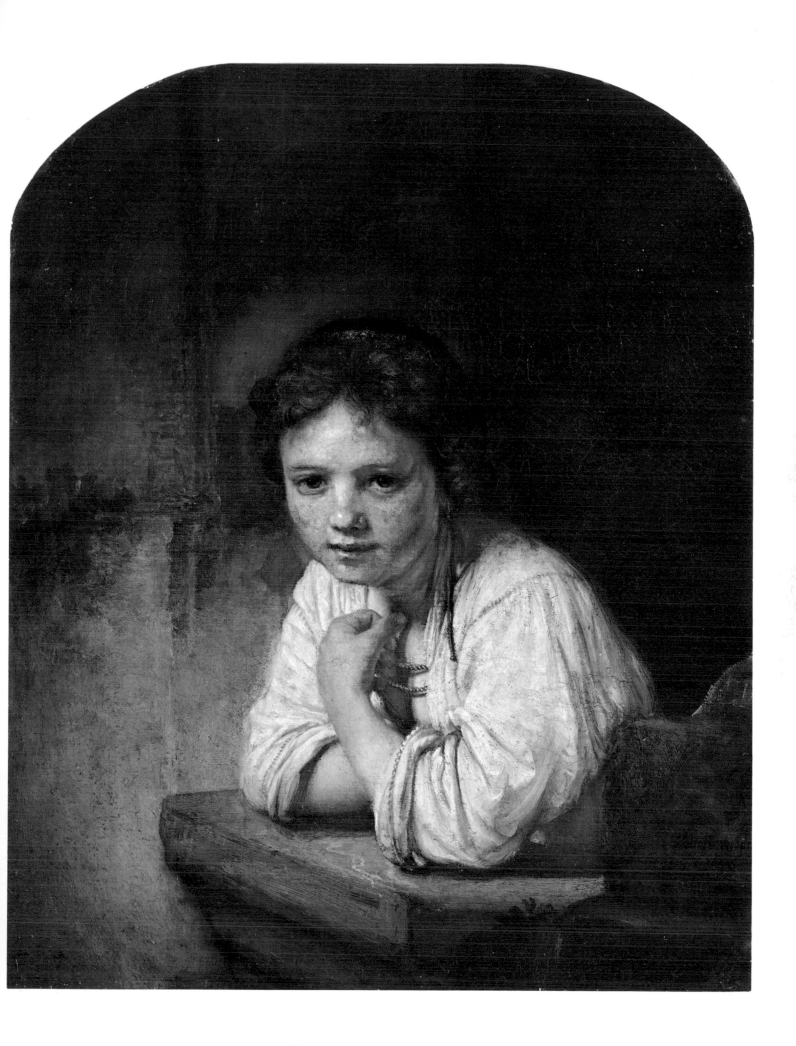

22

The Holy Family with Angels

CANVAS, 117 × 91 CM. SIGNED 'REMBRANDT F. 1645'. LENINGRAD, HERMITAGE

During the 1640s, Rembrandt turned more often than at any other time in his career to the theme of Christ's birth and infancy; he depicted repeatedly, in paintings, drawings and etchings, the Adoration of the Shepherds, the Flight into Egypt and, above all, the Holy Family. The painting of this last subject now in the Hermitage is surely the most tender, the most perfect and the most poetic of them all, and indeed it is one of the most poetic *Holy Families* anywhere in art. Unusually for Rembrandt, angels enter the room: not a swarm of ecstatic grown-up angels, as in Italian baroque art, but a few small boys, at least one of whom, with his wings and arms outstretched, hovers over the cradle with an expression of considerable surprise. In the background, Joseph works away, unconcerned, at his carpentry.

Mary, meanwhile, with a book in her hand, looks up from her reading and turns towards the Child, raising the cover that shields him from the firelight, to gaze at him or perhaps just to make sure he is all right. It is – one cannot avoid the expression – an intensely *human* scene. But no artist in history was more adept than Rembrandt at rendering the spiritual in human terms.

As has been explained in the Introduction, Mary is depicted almost but not quite as an ordinary Dutch peasant girl; not quite, for her features are a little more regular, her face more perfectly oval, than any actual girl's would be, and she wears clothes which hint at the traditional idealized garments of the Madonna as represented in Italian art. The baby and the cradle are in a way more surprising as they are genuinely realistic. The cradle is the handsomest object in the room. The baby, its face as plain as any human baby's, is sound asleep. We rely on Mary, the angels and the overall mood of the picture to tell us that this is a religious scene.

There is a brilliant pen and ink sketch for the painting in Bayonne (Fig. 23; Ben. 567), showing how Rembrandt conceived the composition in almost geometrical terms; in this drawing, to quote Benesch, 'not only solids but rays of light turn into tracks of energetic line'. However, a small oil sketch in an American private collection (Br. 375), which has sometimes been called a study for Mary's head, is now generally thought to be a copy by another artist.

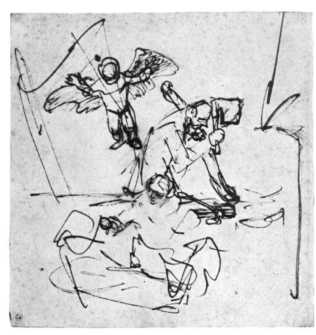

Fig. 23
Study for 'The Holy Family with Angels'

PEN AND BROWN INK, 16.1 × 15.8 CM. C.1645. BAYONNE, MUSÉE BONNAT

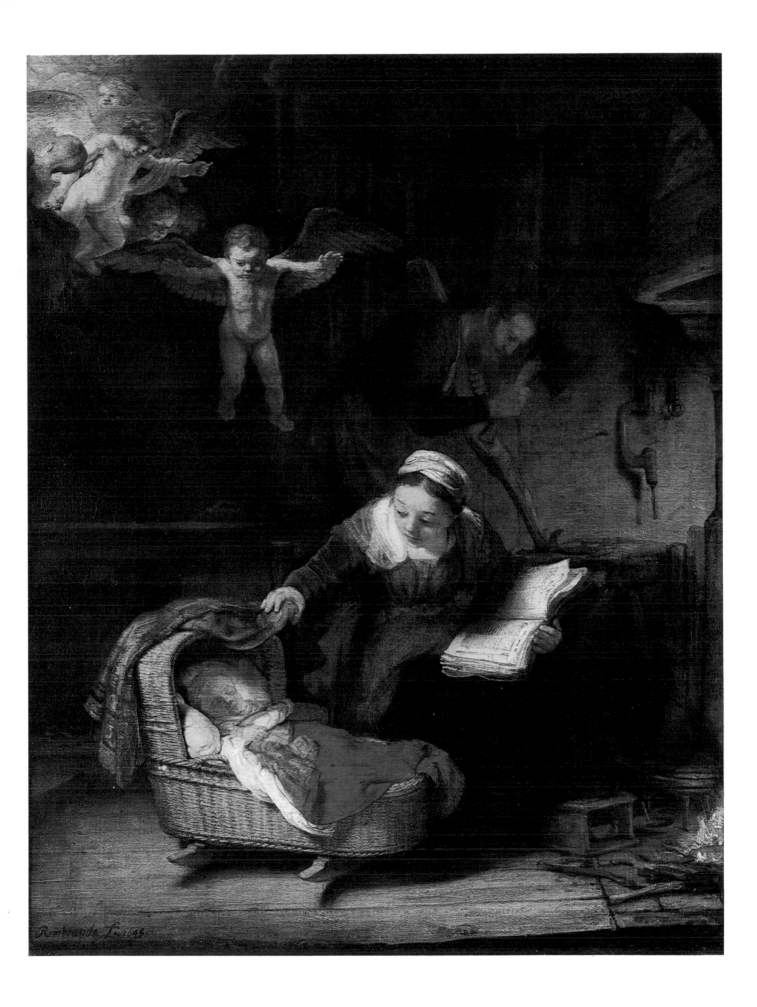

23

The Holy Family with a Cat

PANEL, 46.5 × 68.5 CM. SIGNED 'REMBRANDT FC 1646'. CASSEL, SCHLOSS WILHELMSHÖHE

The remarks in the notes to Plate 22 about the importance of the theme of the Holy Family to Rembrandt in the 1640s also apply to this picture. As might be expected, *The Holy Family with a Cat* is far from being a mere repetition. For one thing, it is more obviously domestic, not to say bourgeois, in mood. The Holy Family is set in just such an interior as Rembrandt himself might have inhabited – and indeed did inhabit, as the drawing of Saskia's lying-in room (Fig. 24) shows. This is not to say that he literally reproduced his own surroundings or that the Madonna and Child are to be understood as portraits of Saskia and one of her children (Saskia had been dead for four years in any case). The painting is not autobiographical in that way. What it shows is how narrow the gap was in Rembrandt's art – never more so than at this stage of his career – between the real and the spiritual: narrow, that is, but also profound. For him, the materials were all there in his drawings from the life of women and children, beggars, artisans, room interiors and furnishings. Yet when put together in his paintings, sweetened and enveloped in light and shade, these materials were transformed into the elements of a religious scene.

The other distinctive feature of this picture is the elaborately de-signed imitation frame and the curtain. How often Rembrandt's paint-ings were in fact framed in this manner is hard to say; to judge from contemporary inventories, probably rather seldom. Plain or perhaps lightly carved black ebony frames seem to have been the rule. Yet on two or three occasions, one example being *The Anatomy Lesson of Doctor Deyman* (Plate 36), Rembrandt sketched a frame of an archi-tectural type round a drawing of the composition, indicating that this was how he would like the painting to be displayed. It added dignity to the work, gave an extra sense of depth to the pictorial space, and gave the picture something of the character of an altarpiece or shrine. The curtain is also a substitute for a real one. In the seventeenth century, curtains were sometimes hung in front of pictures, partly to protect them from dust but chiefly, it seems, to enhance the effect of surprise.

When the curtain was drawn back, the 'marvel' of the work of art seemed all the greater.

All these associations are drawn on by Rembrandt in *The Holy Family with a Cat*. Nor is this the end of it, for the painted frame and curtain are themselves a striking display of illusionism. Illusion is, as it were, employed to emphasize an illusion. Yet because of its style and mood, this is the least showy and artificial of paintings. Its pre-dominant qualities are harmony and repose.

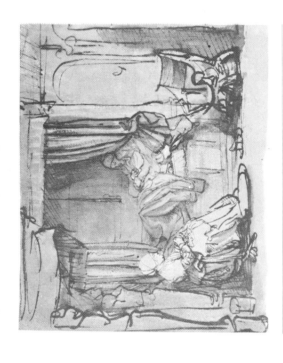

Fig. 24
Saskia's Lying-In Room

PEN AND BROWN INK WITH BROWN AND GREY WASHES, 14.3 × 17.6 CM. C.1640. PARIS, INSTITUT NÉERLANDAIS (FONDATION CUSTODIA)

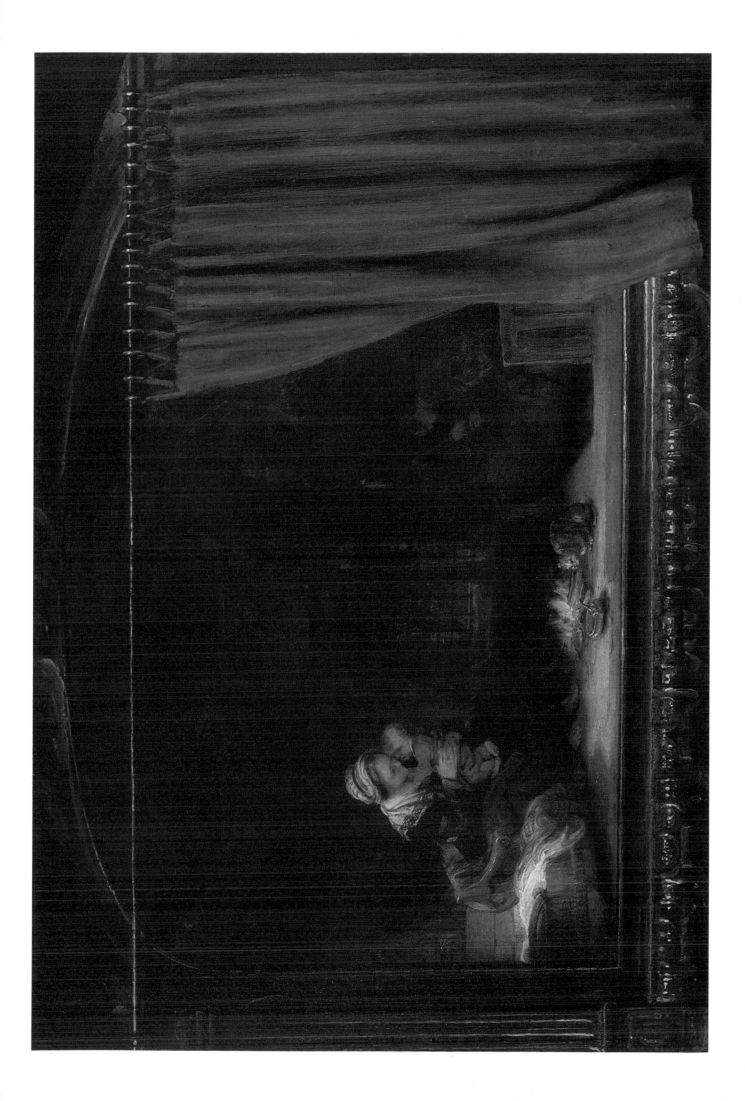

24

Susanna Surprised by the Elders

PANEL, 76 × 91 CM. SIGNED 'REMBRANDT F. 1647'. WEST BERLIN, GEMÄLDEGALERIE

The subject is taken from the Apocryphal History of Susanna. Two Jewish Elders, hidden in the garden, threaten Susanna that they will publicly accuse her of committing adultery with a young man unless she gives herself to them. In contrast to most representations of this theme in art, Rembrandt's painting is not a scene of violence. Susanna's awareness of her dilemma is apparent in her expression as she attempts to cover her nakedness: 'Then Susanna sighed and said, I am straightened on every side: for if I do this thing it is death to me: and if I do it not I cannot escape your hands.' She is eventually exonerated by the wise judge, Daniel, and the Elders are punished.

The subject, like that of Bathsheba, clearly had a considerable fascination for Rembrandt and is evidence (of which there is plenty more elsewhere in his work) that he was a man of strong sensuality. He made numerous drawings of Susanna (such as Fig. 25) and probably at least one other painting, now in The Hague (Br. 505; though some scholars have called this *Bathsheba*). The Hague picture, executed ten years earlier, was used as the starting-point for the present one, which may, in fact, have been begun at about the same time. As X-rays show, the Berlin painting consists of two layers, the first of which reveals the agitated type of composition characteristic of Rem-

brandt's style of the 1630s. When he completed the picture in 1647, he revised the design throughout, changing it into something much calmer. It is now the handling which is lively, not the composition. The figure style, the lighting, the colour and even the relation of the figures to the landscape setting are all typical of the mid-1640s. For the composition, Rembrandt used a painting of *Susanna and the Elders* by Lastman, also now in Berlin, which he copied in a drawing. For all the lack of movement, the narrative and psychological elements of the story are conveyed with the utmost clarity. Rembrandt no longer needed the heightened dramatic language of the Baroque to express emotion at this period of his life.

'A picture of Susanna' was sold by Rembrandt for 500 guilders in 1667, though it is not known if it was this one (no painting of this subject is listed in his inventory of 1656). The present painting was owned by Sir Joshua Reynolds in the eighteenth century.

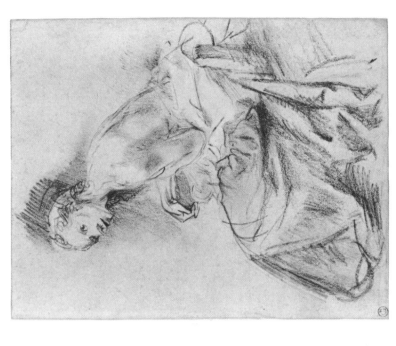

Fig. 25 (right)
Study for 'Susanna Surprised by the Elders'

BLACK CHALK, 20.3 × 16.4 CM. C.1647. WEST BERLIN, KUPFERSTICHKABINETT

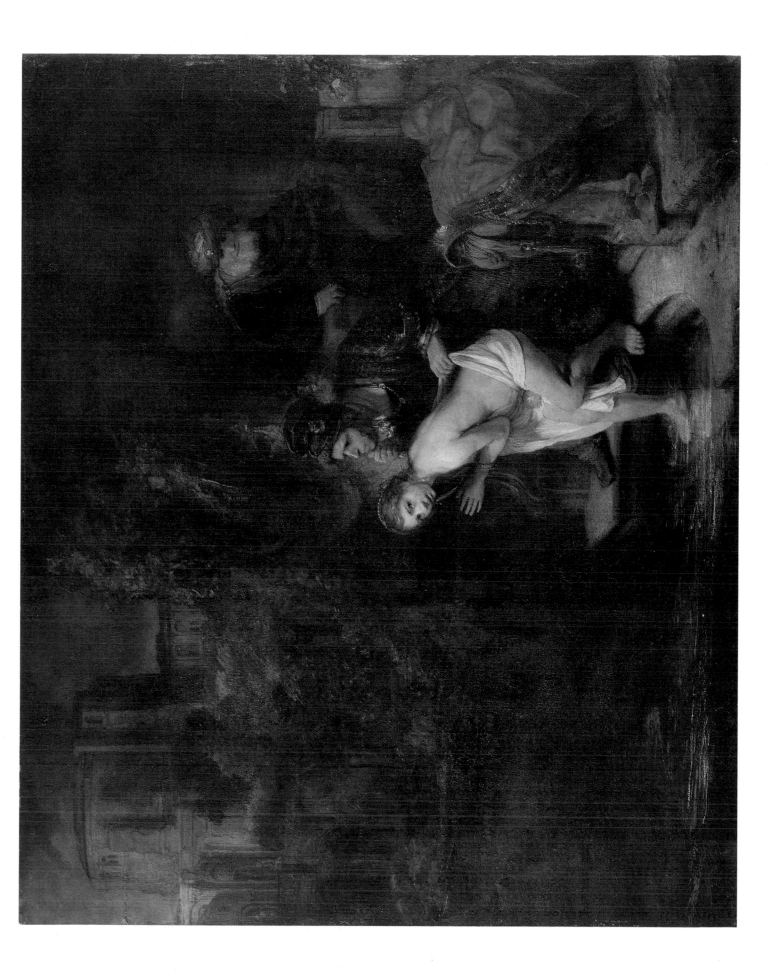

25

Winter Landscape

PANEL, 17 × 23 CM. SIGNED 'REMBRANDT F. 1646'. CASSEL, SCHLOSS WILHELMSHÖHE

For the most part, Rembrandt reserved his direct responses to the flat, open countryside of his native land for his drawings and etchings (Figs. 26 and 27). Very few of his painted landscapes show the same naturalism of approach and, of those that do, the *Winter Landscape* is the only one not to be partly veiled in shadow; though to judge from his inventory of 1656, there may once have been more, for several 'small landscapes' by Rembrandt are listed in it, and one is even described as having been painted from nature. The *Winter Landscape* would not have been painted in this way, as artists did not work out of doors at that time of year, but its small size and broad handling suggest that it was a sketch. It is less decorative than other Dutch *Winter Landscapes* of the period, and the depiction of the weather is startlingly realistic.

However, if a feeling of the open air is the exception in Rembrandt's paintings, it is precisely this quality which is conveyed by his drawings and by many of his etchings. In no other representations of landscape before the nineteenth century is the sensation of actuality so strong. In his drawings especially, Rembrandt's method of composition was very simple and direct. Instead of framing the landscape with trees on one or both sides and opening out a vista in the centre, as was usual at the time, he normally placed the principal subject in the centre middle distance and led the eye to it across an almost empty foreground. Any view into the far distance would occur at the sides. The flatness of the ground is emphasized by a horizontal line across the width of the composition and the subject is set in a plane strictly parallel to the picture surface. (This also applies to the painted *Winter Landscape*.) The subject itself is usually a church, a windmill or farm-buildings with trees. No other visual source, surely, yields so much or such reliable information about the economy of the Dutch countryside in the seventeenth century as Rembrandt's drawings and etchings (see also Fig. 6).

Although some of his landscape etchings are mere finished translations of his drawings into a different medium, others, like *The Goldweigher's Field* (Fig. 27), are more complex. In etching, he was able to take advantage of the fine line produced by the needle, a line considerably finer than any pen-stroke, to render both a greater quantity of detail and a wider effect of space. The etched lines could if necessary be crowded very close together to represent with the utmost clarity both the village in the centre-right middle distance of *The Goldweigher's Field* and the church on the horizon at the left. Alternatively, they could be spaced out a bit more to create the complicated network of dykes and hedgerows in the foreground. When he wanted a broader line, the equivalent of a wash applied with the brush, Rembrandt began at this time to use dry-point, that is, a line scratched with a strong needle directly into the copper plate, not bitten into it by acid. Such a line throws up a burr which traps the ink and so prints the kind of broad, feathery line seen in the immediate foreground of this etching.

The *Goldweigher's Field* obtained its name from the fact that it was supposed to include a view of the country estate, near Naarden, of the Receiver-General (Chief Inspector of Taxes), Jan Uytenbogaert, whose portrait as a 'goldweigher' Rembrandt had etched in 1639. Uytenbogaert had, moreover, come to the artist's aid in the matter of obtaining payment from the Stadholder for the paintings of Christ's Passion (see Plate 13).

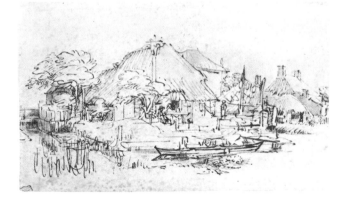

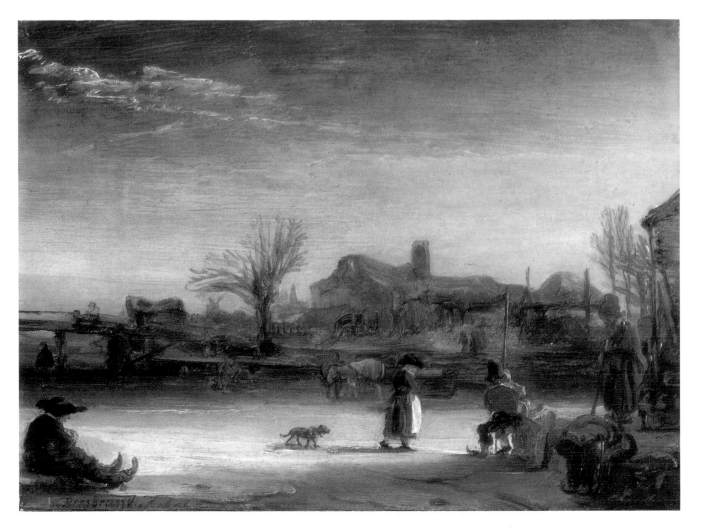

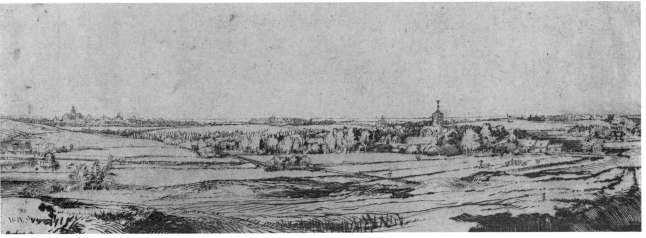

Fig. 26 (left)
Farm Buildings by a River

PEN AND BROWN INK WITH WASH, 14.9 × 24.8 CM. C.1652–3. THE ART
INSTITUTE OF CHICAGO

Fig. 27 (above)
The Goldweigher's Field

ETCHING, 12 × 31.9 CM. SIGNED 'REMBRANDT 1651'. LONDON, BRITISH
MUSEUM

26

Portrait of the Painter, Hendrick Martensz. Sorgh

PANEL, 74 × 67 CM. SIGNED 'REMBRANDT F. 164(7?)'. PRIVATE COLLECTION

In the mid-1640s, the spate of portrait commissions that Rembrandt had received from the wealthy burghers of Amsterdam ever since his arrival in the city slowed down, and only picked up again in the late 1650s. What seems to have happened in this middle decade is that a smoother and more elegant portrait style than Rembrandt's – a style influenced by Van

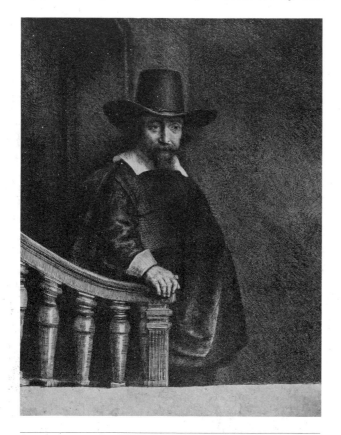

Fig. 28
Portrait of the Jewish Physician, Ephraim Bonus

ETCHING, 24 × 17.7 CM. SIGNED 'REMBRANDT F. 1647', LONDON.
BRITISH MUSEUM

Dyck and practised in Amsterdam chiefly by Bartholomaeus van der Helst (see Fig. 43) – captured the market, though the possibility should not be overlooked that Rembrandt himself took a decision not to compete in this market for the time being. Those clients who now sat to him for their portraits were drawn not so much from high society as from a circle of doctors, preachers, print-sellers and fellow artists whom he probably knew personally. His *Portrait of Hendrick Martensz. Sorgh* (*c.*1611–70), who was a minor painter of peasant scenes living in Rotterdam, is a particularly fine example of this. The figure, with black moustache, beard and hair and dressed entirely in black apart from his plain white collar, is modelled with the utmost firmness. Face, expression and silhouette are all equally strong. The handling is broad and the lighting simple. There is none of the formal complexity or dwelling on detail that occurs in Rembrandt's earlier portraits. The sitter gazes directly, almost fiercely, at the observer. Using a slightly softer style, Rembrandt painted a companion portrait of Sorgh's wife (Br. 370), which still hangs beside it in the same collection.

A similar pictorial approach is seen in the contemporary etched portrait of *Ephraim Bonus* (Fig. 28). For this work, Rembrandt used the medium in a manner which imitates oil painting, that is, the lines made by the needle are employed entirely to create light and shade; they do not exist as lines in their own right, as in *The Goldweigher's Field*, or serve as contour lines enclosing forms. This was a new role for etching, which brought it close to the recently invented art of mezzotint (though Rembrandt did not continue etching for long in this style). An oil sketch for the etching is in the Rijksmuseum (Br. 252), which further emphasizes the connection between the print and oil painting. Ephraim Bonus, or Buëno, was a famous physician of Portuguese-Jewish origin living in Amsterdam.

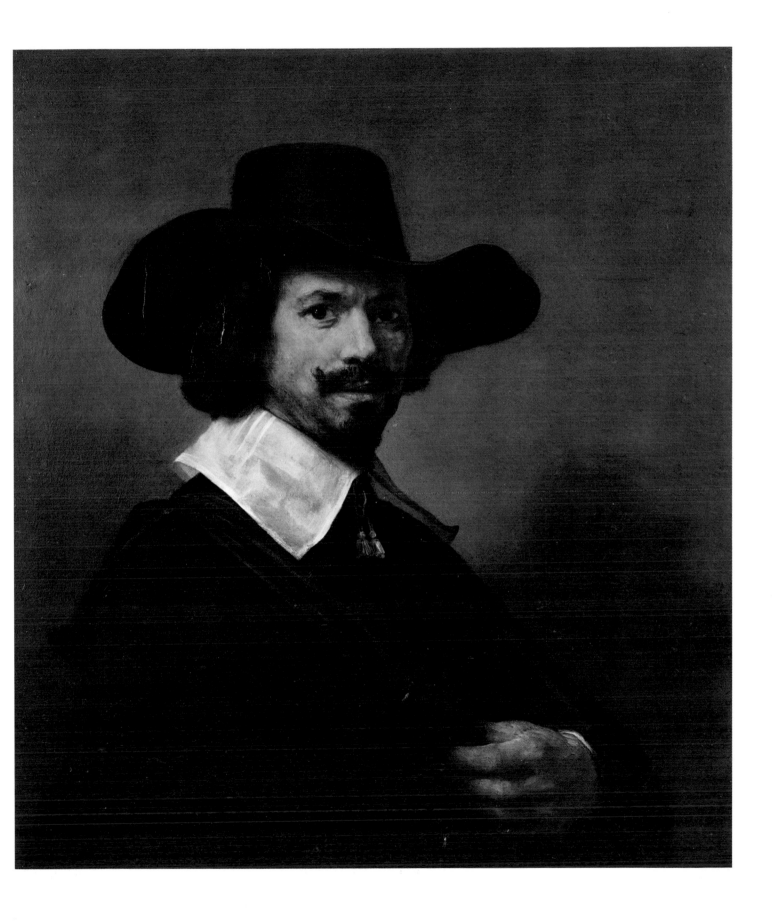

27

Head of Christ

PANEL, 25 × 20 CM. C.1645–50. WEST BERLIN, GEMÄLDEGALERIE

This is one of a series of small oil studies of the head of Christ painted by Rembrandt in the late 1640s. All were done from the same model, although the features are varied slightly. The face is given a Jewish appearance, clearly differentiating it from the conception of Christ seen elsewhere in European art. Its characteristics are narrow cheeks, wide-set eyes, a thick black beard and dark hair parted low over the forehead. The lips are slightly open and the eyes have a sorrowful, yearning expression.

There is a manifest connection in mood here with *The Hundred Guilder Print* (Fig. 29). This famous etching, one of Rembrandt's largest, owes its popular title to the fact that an impression of if was sold in the late seventeenth century for the then large sum of 100 guilders. Its real subject is Christ healing the sick and receiving the little children. Such a concentration on Christ's love for human beings is typical of Rembrandt in this decade, and he makes Christ the still centre of a complex and crowded, though not turbulent, composition. The figures of the sick and poor recall the studies Rembrandt had made from nature during the preceding ten years (see Fig. 21), and he may well have begun work on this print not long after 1640. The figure of Christ in its present form may have been the final insertion, and there are signs that his position was once different. So simply designed a figure, with the body turned directly towards the observer, might well be contemporary with this oil study of Christ's head.

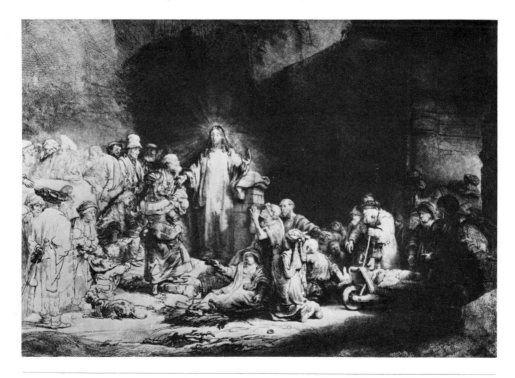

Fig. 29
The Hundred Guilder Print

ETCHING, 27.8 × 39.6 CM. C.1642–6. LONDON, BRITISH MUSEUM

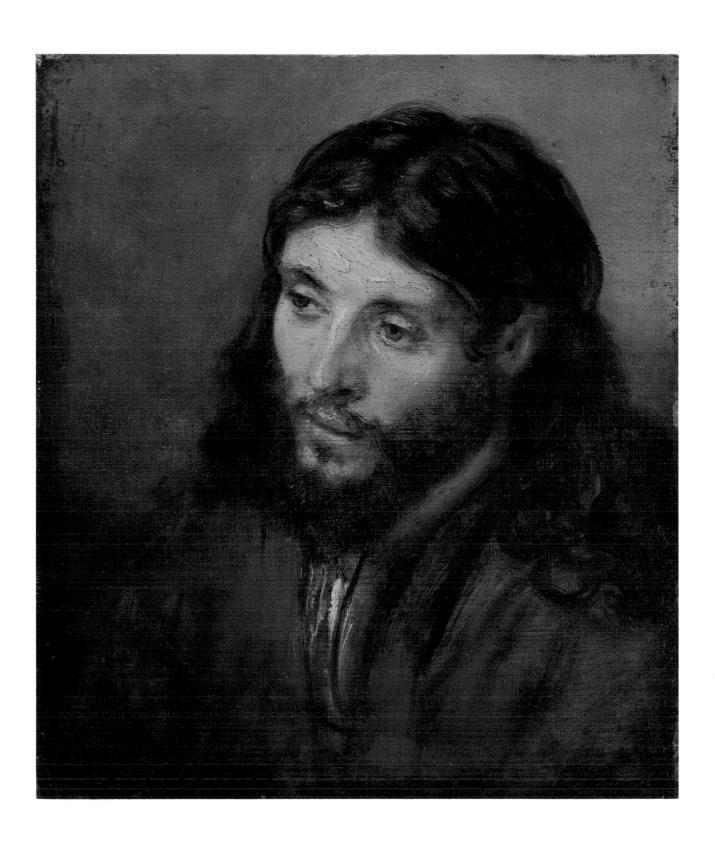

28

Aristotle Contemplating the Bust of Homer

CANVAS, 143.5 × 136.5 CM. SIGNED 'REMBRANDT F. 1653'. NEW YORK, METROPOLITAN MUSEUM OF ART

Rembrandt painted this impressive if unusual picture for the Sicilian collector, Don Antonio Ruffo of Messina (1610–78). It is one of the few works by him known to have been commissioned by a foreign patron. Ruffo, who never travelled and who formed his collection through dealers and by correspondence, would have heard of Rembrandt through his contacts in Italy, where the artist had a considerable reputation for his etchings. Besides *Aristotle Contemplating the Bust of Homer*, he commissioned two further pictures from Rembrandt and bought a large group of his etchings in 1669.

Interestingly, Rembrandt chose the subjects of the paintings himself, and when the *Aristotle* first arrived in Messina Ruffo was uncertain what it represented. He called it a 'Half figure of a philosopher ... it seems to be an Aristotle or an Albertus Magnus' (who was a medieval follower of Aristotle). It was only in the course of the negotiations over Rembrandt's second two pictures during 1661 that the true subject emerged. However, Ruffo was delighted with the *Aristotle* and even agreed to pay Rembrandt's enormous price which, as he pointed out, was far more than an Italian painter would have charged. The other two pictures caused trouble on account of their condition, but no fault was found with their style or subject-matter. These two pictures were an *Alexander the Great* (possibly the painting now in the Gulbenkian Foundation, Lisbon; Br. 479) and a *Homer Teaching* (now, cut down, in the Mauritshuis; Br. 483), and Rembrandt wrote that all three should be hung together, with *Alexander the Great* in the middle.

Beyond recognizing the identities of the two persons represented in the *Aristotle Contemplating the Bust of Homer*, scholars have speculated for some time over its deeper meaning and over the relationship to it of the other two paintings. (J. Held's *Rembrandt's 'Aristotle' and Other Rembrandt Studies*, 1969, contains the most extensive investigation.) Nothing quite like this picture had ever been painted before. Aristotle is a comparatively rare subject in art, and there was no agreed likeness of him surviving from antiquity (the most famous earlier representation of him in painting is in Raphael's *School of Athens*). What is more, no precedent existed for the portrait of a historical figure accompanied by a classical bust, though portraits of living scholars with

busts beside them and books elsewhere in the picture are fairly common. Rembrandt drew on the conventions of this type of work for his image of Aristotle, substituting a gowned, bearded and somewhat magician-like imaginary figure for the portrait of a living individual. Aristotle is dressed neither in classical garments nor in modern clothing but in a white-ish, wide-sleeved gown which Rembrandt evidently kept in his studio and which he used later for a painting sometimes said to be *Hendrickje Stoffels as Flora* (Br. 114). The long black 'apron' may be a pure invention. Over one shoulder Aristotle wears a heavy gold chain of honour, with a medallion, possibly representing Athena, the goddess of wisdom, attached to it. The model for the figure was the same as for the *Bearded Man with a Cap* in the National Gallery London, (Br. 283). The bust was copied from a well-known classical bust of Homer, of which Rembrandt may have owned a version or a cast. Busts of both Homer and Aristotle are listed as successive items in his inventory of 1656 (though there is no record of what they looked like), and their presence side by side in his gallery, or *Kunst Caemer*, may have supplied the initial impulse for the picture.

As to the picture's deeper meaning, it may be unwise to seek too far. Two treatises associated with Aristotle perhaps offer a clue. One is his *Poetics*, in which he reveals his admiration for Homer above all other poets. The other is the *Physiognomics*, though that is now thought to be spurious. Physiognomics is the study of the relationship between physical appearance, on the one hand, and intelligence and character, on the other, and, if this is alluded to, Aristotle's hand on Homer's skull in the painting would be an appropriate motif. It is interesting that the Italian artist, Guercino, who was at one time asked by Ruffo to paint a companion piece to the *Aristotle* and was sent a drawing of the picture, thought that it represented a physiognomist.

Rembrandt's choice of subject in the other two pictures may be equally straightforward. Alexander the Great had been tutored by Aristotle as a boy and he, too, was a great admirer of Homer. The living Homer as teacher would thus have been a suitable subject with which to conclude the series, a series which, in general, is a celebration of the greatest of ancient Greek poets.

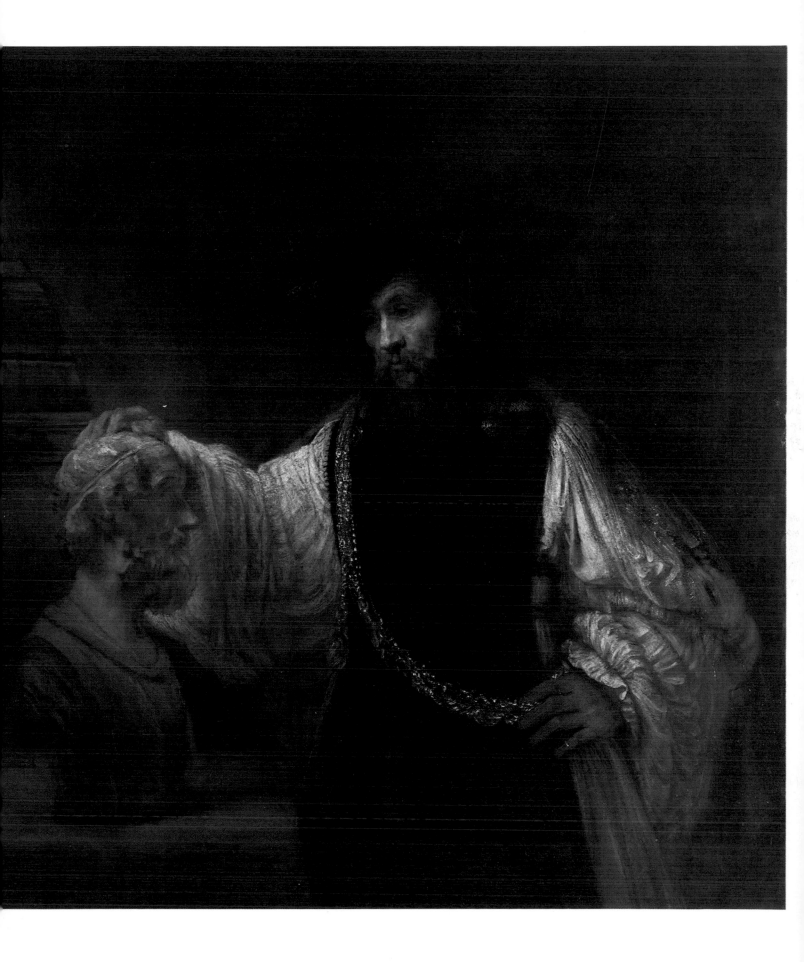

29

Portrait of Hendrickje Stoffels

CANVAS, 100 × 83.5 CM. SIGNED (FALSELY?) 'REMBRANDT F. 1659 (?)'. LONDON, NATIONAL GALLERY

Unlike Saskia, of whom Rembrandt made an in-scribed portrait-drawing (Fig. 13), Hendrickje Stof-fels is nowhere explicitly identified in his art. How-ever, there exist up to half-a-dozen portraits of an attractive, round-faced woman, showing her at dif-ferent ages, painted during the period when Hen-drickje lived with Rembrandt as his mistress, and these are generally agreed to be of her. They reveal an affection and degree of intimacy between artist and sitter that would be inconceivable in a commissioned portrait, and at the same time the face is too strongly characterized for it to be that of an anonymous model, like the *Young Girl Leaning on a Window-Sill* (Plate 21).

Hendrickje Stoffels is first mentioned as a member of Rembrandt's household in a document of 1 October 1649. She was then about twenty-three. She bore him a daughter, Cornelia, in 1654 and remained with him until her death in 1663. Rembrandt never married her, presumably because a second marriage would have deprived him of the much-needed in-come from Saskia's dowry, held in trust under the terms of her will for their son, Titus. Besides sitting to Rembrandt for her portrait, Hendrickje may have modelled for him on various occasions, as, for ex-ample, for the *Woman Bathing* (Plate 30) and, very probably, *Bathsheba* (Fig. 31).

The date of the National Gallery portrait has caused problems, and modern scholars consider that both the signature and date on this canvas may be later additions. Some time in the first half of the 1650s seems to be the most likely date on stylistic grounds. The picture shows the increasing breadth of form and handling characteristic of Rembrandt's style in this period. The forms have lost that complexity of struc-ture and quantity of surface detail which they had earlier in his career, while remaining firm and block-like, not flattened out as they were to become by 1660. The dark red shape at the bottom, which is hard to interpret, may have been added at the last moment to give the composition a foreground, after Rembrandt had changed the position of Hen-drickje's hands, which X-rays show were originally folded on her lap.

The portrait is one of the most private in all Rem-brandt's work. It is very quiet and dignified in mood but also sensuous, even sensual, in feeling. A hundred years ago, when it was in an English private col-lection, the German scholar, Wilhelm von Bode, praised 'the indescribable expression of feminine charm' which it evokes. It is appropriate to ac-company this beautiful portrait with an illustration of a contemporary self-portrait drawing of Rembrandt (Fig. 30) in studio attire. Equally forthright and equ-ally bold and simple in style, it epitomizes the image that Hendrickje would have had of him as he painted her.

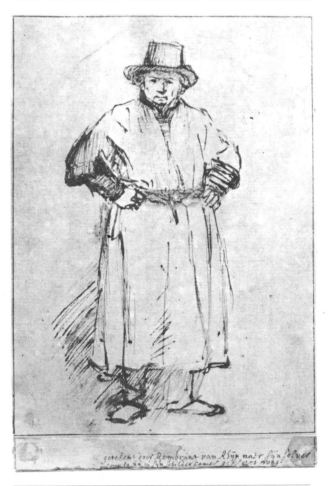

Fig. 30
Self-Portrait in Studio Attire

PEN AND BROWN INK, 20.3 × 13.4 CM. C.1655. AMSTERDAM, REMBRANDT-HUIS

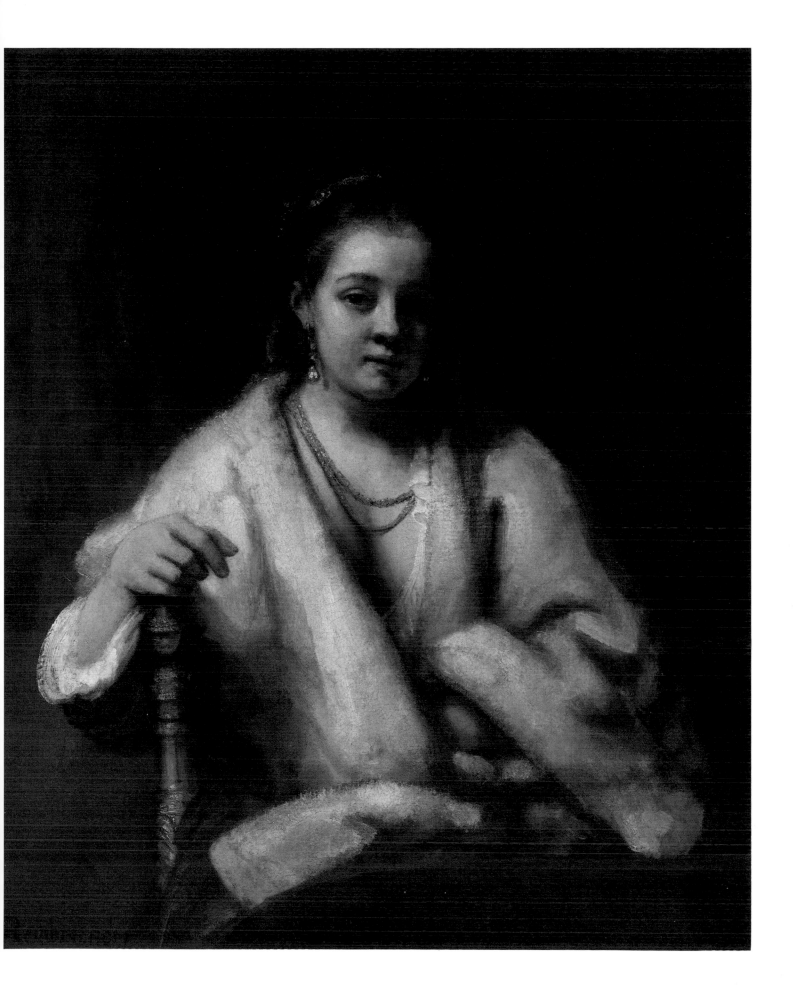

30

A Woman Bathing

PANEL, 61.8 × 47 CM. SIGNED 'REMBRANDT F 1654 (OR 1655)'. LONDON, NATIONAL GALLERY

Because the face is similar to that in Plate 29 and other portraits of her, it has been plausibly suggested that Hendrickje Stoffels was the model here too. There are overtones in this picture of the biblical subject of either *Bathsheba* (Fig. 31) or *Susanna and the Elders* (Plate 24); this much is made clear by the heavy gold and red cloak behind the figure and by the grotto-like setting. At least in these areas, Rembrandt was seeking to create a poetic effect. Still, as is so often the case in his work, the dividing line between a religious subject and a product of the artist's fancy, with no particular subject intended, is a fine one. The young woman appears completely absorbed in her bathe and shows no sign of the reactions appropriate to either Susanna or Bathsheba. It is possible that Rembrandt had one or other of these subjects subconsciously in mind when painting the picture while not specifically intending to illustrate either; or if he did so intend, he failed to make the fact clear. As a work of art, the picture has all the characteristics of an independent study, or a sketch made for its own sake, and the figure, if not the background, was evidently painted from life. The brushstrokes are dashing and impulsive, suggesting rather than defining the forms; except in the head and flesh-parts of the figure, no attention at all is paid to detail. The abiding impression is one of spontaneity and freedom. However, Rembrandt signed and dated the picture and may have sold it or hoped to sell it.

The large finished painting of Bathsheba (Fig. 31), though of the same date, is very different. The relationship between form and content here is close and highly expressive. Bathsheba, the beautiful wife of Uriah the Hittite, was washing herself when she was spied by King David from the roof of his palace; he sent messengers to say he desired her, and she consented and went in to him (2 Samuel, Chapter XI). Rembrandt shows her with mingled feelings of regret, submission and anticipation as she sits, holding the King's letter loosely in her hand and pondering the implications of his command. Her pose and that of the woman drying her feet (who discreetly averts her gaze) are taken from an engraving after a classical relief, probably representing a bride being prepared for her wedding-night, and this is also in part how Bathsheba herself is depicted. The intrusion of any other figures into the composition, either King David or the messengers, would have been superfluous. The subject in all its aspects is fully realized as it is. The use by Rembrandt of the classical relief gives the design an appropriate and haunting calm. Whether or not he painted the figure from the life is hard to say, but the shape and weight of Hendrickje's body must have been in his mind. The outcome is one of the most profound comments on sexuality in the history of art.

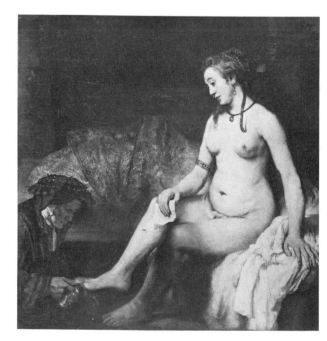

Fig. 31
Bathsheba Holding King David's Letter

CANVAS, 142 × 142 CM. SIGNED 'REMBRANDT FT. 1654'. PARIS, MUSÉE DU LOUVRE

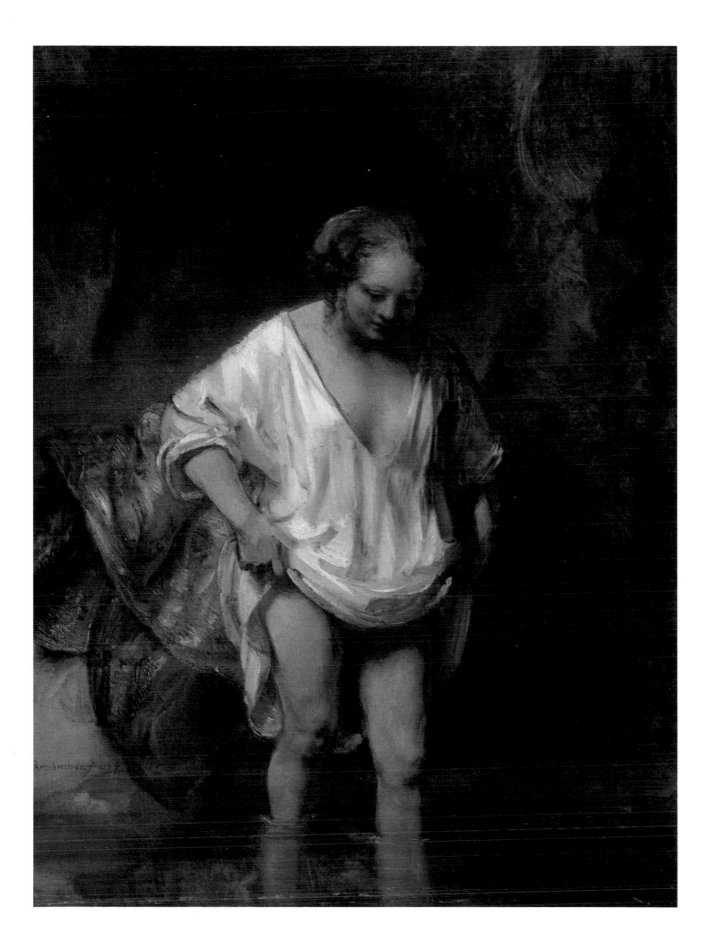

31

Portrait of Titus

CANVAS, 77 × 63 CM. SIGNED 'REMBRANDT F. 1655'. ROTTERDAM, MUSEUM BOYMANS-VAN BEUNINGEN

This is probably the earliest identifiable portrait of Rembrandt's son, Titus (1641–68). He was the last child born to Saskia and the only one to survive infancy. As with Hendrickje, there are no documented portraits of him, but about four or five portraits of the same boy are known, painted between 1655 and about 1662, and it would be unreasonable to doubt that they represent Titus. Rembrandt also made a number of drawings of him and may have used him as a model for religious pictures. Titus himself grew up to be an artist and several of his drawings have been identified. From 1660 he acted as his father's dealer but died as a young man in 1668, the year before Rembrandt himself.

What is slightly curious about the Boymans Museum picture is that Titus appears to be represented as a younger boy than he actually was. Shown seated, or perhaps standing, at a desk and puzzling over his homework, he has the large eyes, rounded cheeks and small mouth of a child of eight or nine, rather than those of a boy of his true age, which was fourteen. Perhaps Rembrandt, looking at him one day, recalled him as a child and painted him accordingly. Be that as it may, the portrait is delightfully fresh and spontaneous. For all the advancing mysteriousness of Rembrandt's art, his style could still encompass something quite simple. The same relaxed and observant mood can be seen in his several drawings of lions (Fig. 32) of about this date.

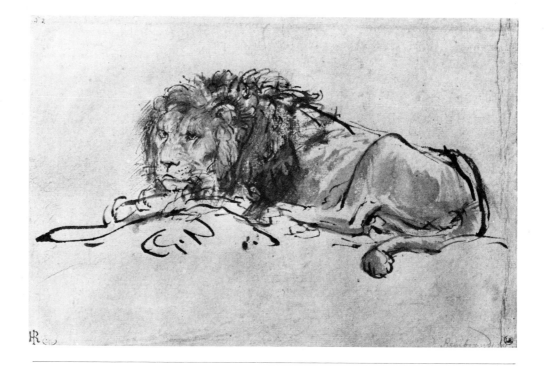

Fig. 32
A Lion Resting

DRAWN WITH THE BRUSH AND PERHAPS ALSO WITH A REED-PEN, 13.8 × 20.7 CM. C.1651–2. PARIS, MUSÉE DU LOUVRE

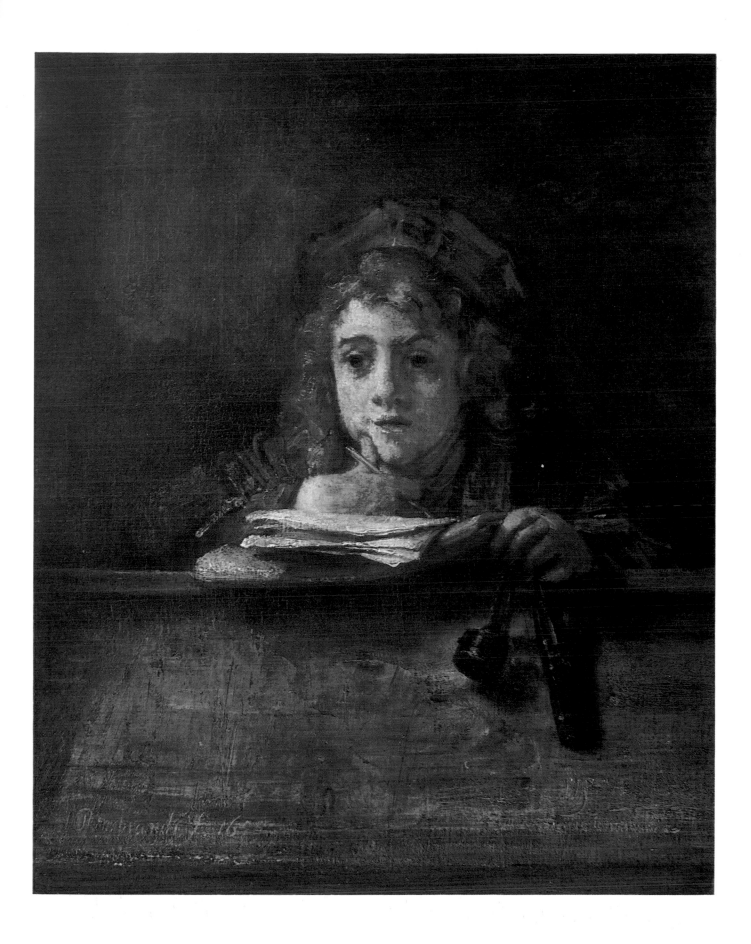

32

Portrait of Jan Six

CANVAS, 112 × 102 CM. 1654. AMSTERDAM, SIX COLLECTION

At a time when commissions from the *haute bour-geoisie* were few and far between (see Plate 26), Rembrandt painted, in this portrait of the wealthy magistrate, man of letters and connoisseur, Jan Six, one of his greatest masterpieces of the genre. The sitter wears a long, buttoned coat in the latest fashion with, over one shoulder, a heavy, gold-braided red cloak. He draws on his gloves and looks slightly questioningly towards the observer, as if he has been accosted when on the point of leaving the house. The fact that the figure is placed a little to one side of the canvas enhances this effect, as it gives him room to move. Yet while there is a hint of the instantaneous in this portrait, the artist's interpretation generally is restrained and dignified. The low viewpoint, allowing little space between the top of the hat and the frame, combined with the width of the clothes, produce an image of controlled power. The shadow cast over the upper part of the face by the hat is another effective pictorial device; by encouraging the observer to read more into the eyes than is actually defined by the paint, it makes the sitter's expression seem more alert while his personality remains inscrutable. A similar blend of the qualities of vivacity and mysteriousness is created by the background shadows which cut repeatedly into the figure. At the same time, Rembrandt was never more direct or more vigorous in his handling of paint. Within the outline of the form, the different parts of the clothing are defined by sharp, straight edges; in particular, the two collars, the braid, the tassels at the throat and the open coat-sleeve are treated in this way. The same is to some extent true of the hands and parts of the face. The braid on the cloak is simply suggested by repeated strokes of a broad brush half-charged with yellow paint applied on top of the red. The brushwork is at its most lively, however, in the area of the hands and gloves (detail, Fig. 33), where the forms themselves are less regular and there is a suggestion of movement.

Jan Six (1618–1700) came from a successful merchant family but took up a career as a magistrate and devoted himself to literature, collecting and travel.

He was burgomaster of Amsterdam in 1691. Rembrandt got to know him at the latest by 1647, when he etched Six's portrait, and in the following year he provided an illustration for the latter's drama, *Medea* (M. 270). The two men probably remained on friendly terms until the year after the portrait discussed here was painted, when the relationship broke down. It seems that Six was less accommodating than some of Rembrandt's other acquaintances when the artist got into financial difficulties. The date of this portrait is established by a cryptic verse-couplet which Six wrote about it, in which the capital letters, when read as Roman numerals, add up to 1654.

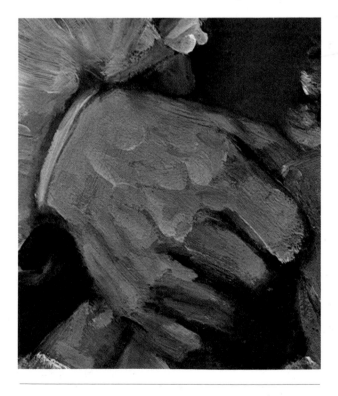

Fig. 33
Detail from the 'Portrait of Jan Six'

SEE PLATE 32

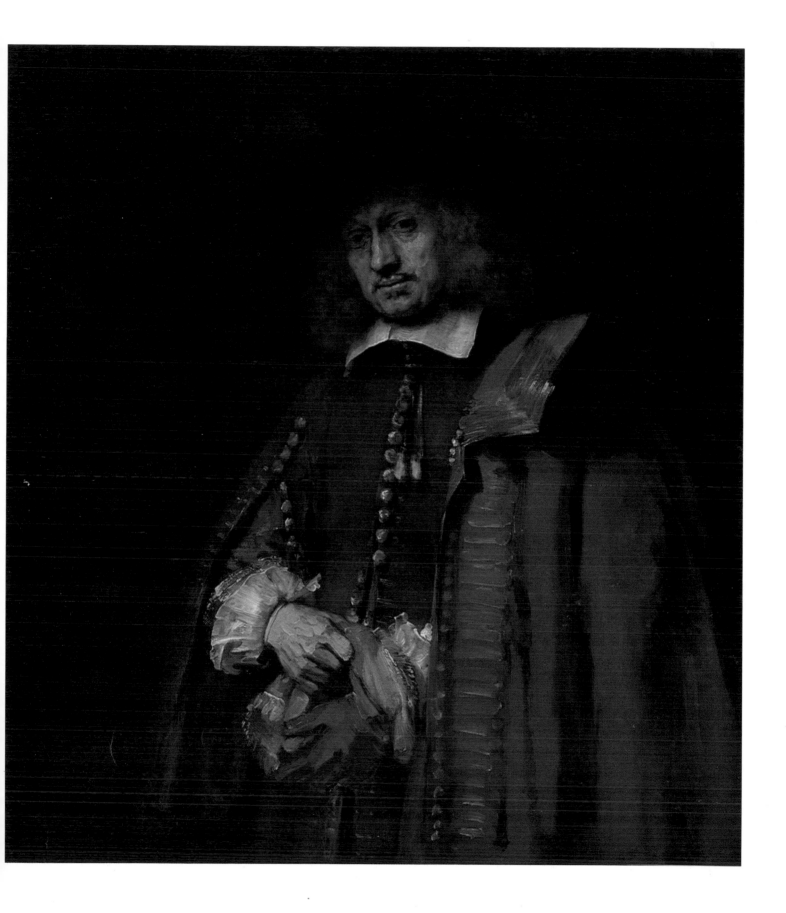

33

An Old Woman Reading

CANVAS, 79 × 65 CM. SIGNED 'REMBRANDT F. 1655'. REPRODUCED BY COURTESY OF HIS GRACE THE DUKE OF BUCCLEUCH AND QUEENSBERRY, K.T.

A single figure reading or writing is a common motif in Rembrandt's work. The device served to provide a focus of interest within the picture without disturbing the atmosphere of calm. Further, it turned a figure-painting partly into a subject picture. The principal feature of this *Old Woman Reading* is the concentration of light in the centre. It is not just a pale tone or a piece of white clothing but a positive glow. Light enters the picture space in some unexplained way from above and it is then reflected off the book on

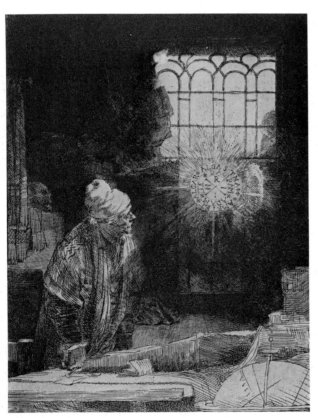

Fig. 34
Faust in his Study

ETCHING, 20.9 × 16.1 CM. C.1653. LONDON, BRITISH MUSEUM

to the woman's dress and face. She wears a similar head-scarf to that worn by the old woman in Plate 5, and in some ways this is a revised version of that picture. The treatment of form, however, is now much simpler and broader, the composition is almost symmetrical and the figure is posed in a frontal view. None of this would have occurred to Rembrandt in his early period. The same woman posed for two or three other paintings by him in the mid-1650s.

The 'Faust' etching (Fig. 34) also has as its main ingredients a single figure, books and a gleam of light in an interior. There is the same use of strong, simple lines in the construction of the composition. But whereas the *Old Woman Reading* represents an ordinary subject transformed into a compelling and Sibyl-like image, the 'Faust' etching deals explicitly in the supernatural. Whatever the true subject is, it is almost certainly not Faust, or at any rate not the legendary Dr Faustus who sold his soul to the devil in return for the knowledge that would make him master of the universe. The disc of light with letters which appears inside the window in Rembrandt's etching has been shown to be based on an amulet, or charm, though the meaning of the letters, apart from INRI (*Jesus Nazarenus Rex Judaeorum*), has not yet been discovered. The apparition, which is accompanied by a hand pointing to a mirror, is clearly intended as a source of inspiration to the scholar who gazes at it. Yet what scholar is he? One suggestion is that the etching has to do with the doctrines of Socinianism, which was a Protestant heresy proscribed even in The Netherlands, as its principal tenet was a denial of the divinity of Christ. On this reckoning, the scholar might be Faustus Socinus, one of the two sixteenth-century Italian theologians who founded the sect.

However that may be, the etching had acquired its familiar title, *Faust in his Study*, by the middle of the eighteenth century and as such it inspired Goethe, who used a copy of it as the frontispiece to his *Faust*, Part I, published in 1790. The modern idea of Faust as a gowned scholar conceiving his longings for power and riches in a darkened study owes its origins, through Goethe, to Rembrandt's etching.

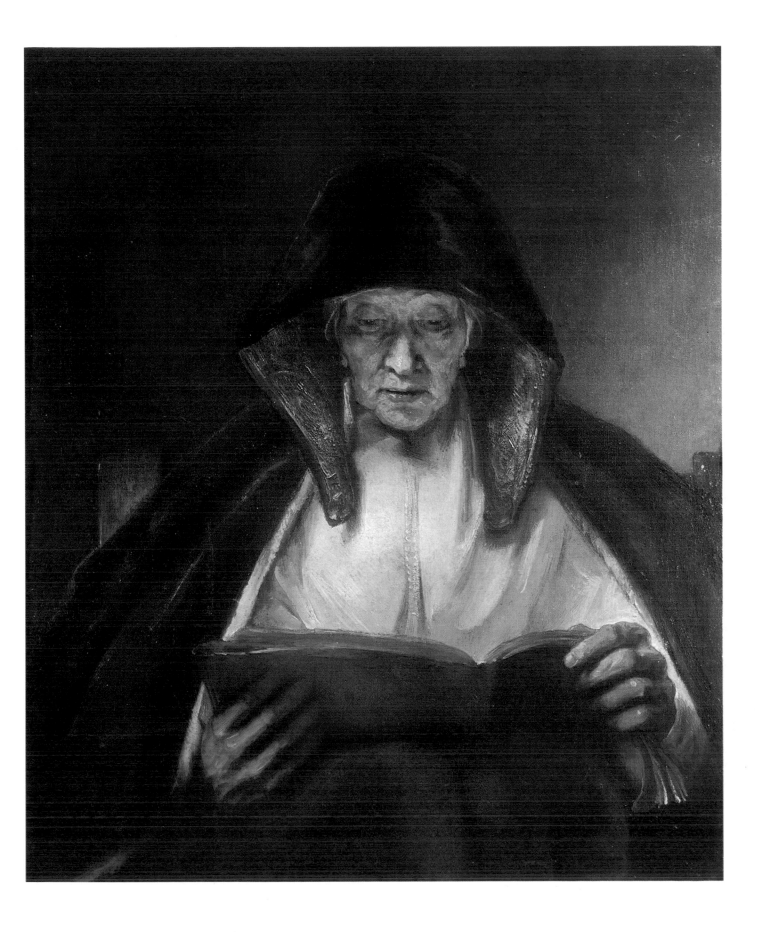

34

The Polish Rider

CANVAS, 115 × 135 CM. SIGNED 'RE...'. C.1655. NEW YORK, FRICK COLLECTION

The subject of this picture, perhaps the most poetic and curious of all Rembrandt's representations of a single figure, has given rise to much speculation. Almost the only thing not in doubt is its date, which for reasons of style is generally agreed to be about 1655. The painting is not obviously either a representation of a real or imaginary historical character, a portrait of a contemporary, or a genre study, although it has elements suggestive of all three. It was first described in a letter written in 1791, probably from Amsterdam or The Hague, as 'a Cossack on Horseback' (A. Ciechanowiecki, *Art Bulletin*, XLII, 1960); it may thus have already been known by that title in The Netherlands in the eighteenth century. The writer was an agent of the King of Poland, for whom he bought the picture, and it remained in that country throughout the nineteenth century. The figure was then called an officer of the Lisowski regiment, a famous Polish cavalry unit which fought in Western Europe during the Thirty Years War (however, this regiment was disbanded in 1636, twenty years before the date of the picture). The title *The Polish Rider* was finally given by Henry Clay Frick when he bought the painting from a private collection in Poland in 1910.

Modern criticism began with a long article by J. Held in the *Art Bulletin*, XXVI, 1944 (reprinted with modifications in *Rembrandt's 'Aristotle' and Other Rembrandt Studies*, 1969). He maintained that the costume and weapons were not specifically Polish but were broadly Eastern European, perhaps with some Turkish elements, which Rembrandt evolved partly from his imagination, partly from the collection of old clothes and accoutrements which he kept in his studio and partly from engravings. Held suggested that Rembrandt conceived the painting as a generalized image of the Christian Soldier, on the lines of Dürer's engraving of *The Knight, Death and the Devil* (although the meaning of this is itself uncertain). Valentiner, too, thought that the figure was an invented one (*Art Quarterly*, XI, 1948). He saw it as an imaginary portrait of the medieval Dutch hero, Gysbrecht van Aemstel, who visited Poland at one time in his career. Yet another suggestion, recently put forward by Colin Campbell, is that the painting represents the biblical subject of the Prodigal Son setting forth to spend his inheritance.

In the meantime, however, the traditional idea that the rider is a Polish cavalry officer of the seventeenth century was revived. Writing in 1965 and drawing on a wider range of comparative engravings and surviving costumes and weapons of the period than were originally available to Held, Z. Zygulski (*Bulletin du Musée National de Varsovie*, VI) argued strongly that Rembrandt painted the costumed figure from life. This suggestion is persuasive, if still not proved, and is borne out by the precision and consistency with which the details of the clothes and weapons are painted; they do not look 'faked'. Moreover, if Zygulski is correct, the evidence that the picture may have been known as 'a Cossack on Horseback' in The Netherlands in the eighteenth century gains added significance; it could be a title which went back to Rembrandt's lifetime. Polish cavalrymen were fairly often to be seen in Western Europe during the seventeenth century, and it would be characteristic of Rembrandt, with his love of the picturesque and the exotic, to have painted one.

Even so, the painting does not seem quite to be a portrait in the sense that, say, Rembrandt's only other single equestrian figure, the so-called *Frederik Rihel* of c.1663 in the National Gallery, London, is a portrait. Although the pose of *The Polish Rider* with hand on hip and his head turned towards the observer belongs to a portrait-type, the treatment of the face is too indefinite for it to be the outcome of a portrait commission. The fact that the figure is only half life-size also speaks against this explanation. Above all, the landscape and the mood of the painting as a whole breathe, as all critics are agreed, an unforgettable air of mystery. The landscape has a spaciousness differentiating it from a conventional portrait backdrop. It includes a castle on a mountain in the distance and a stream in the foreground, which the horse and rider are about to ford. The emaciated horse with its alert rider paces soundlessly through this landscape, its hooves barely touching the ground. Some narrative content seems to be hinted at. Yet no clue or symbol is visible which might allow us to identify a subject, nor is the costume (if it is indeed actual and contemporary) easily reconcilable with the notion that the painting is either a subject picture or an imaginary portrait of a historical character.

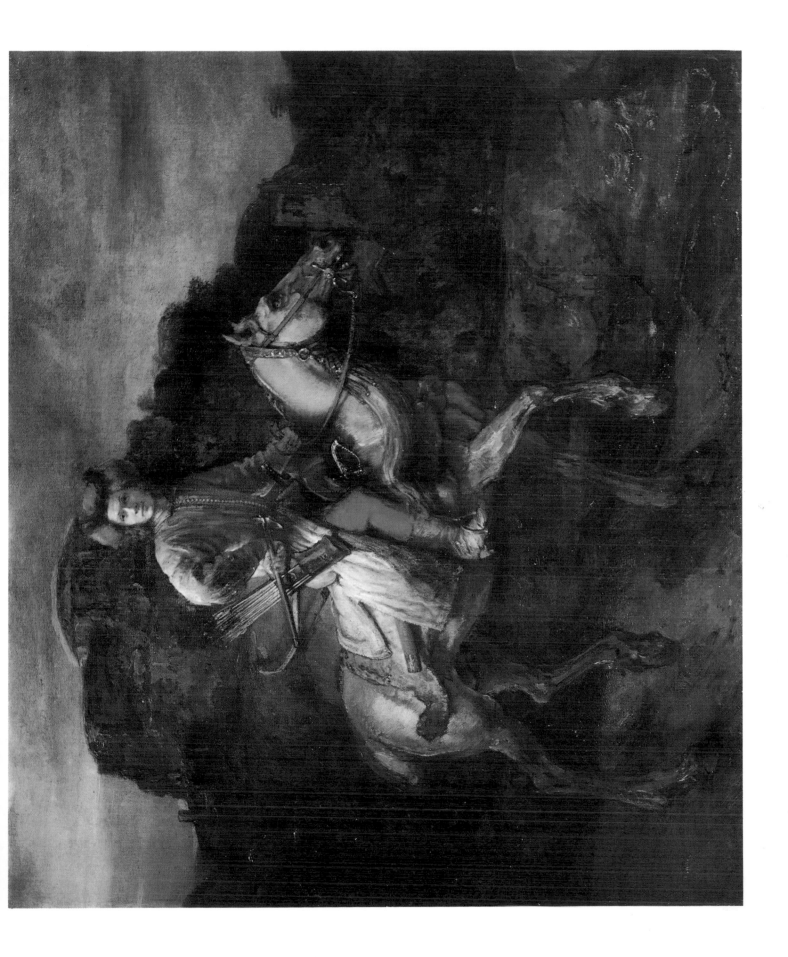

35

Jacob Blessing the Children of Joseph

CANVAS, 175.5 × 210.5 CM. FALSELY SIGNED 'RIMBRAN… F. 1656'. CASSEL, SCHLOSS WILHELMSHÖHE

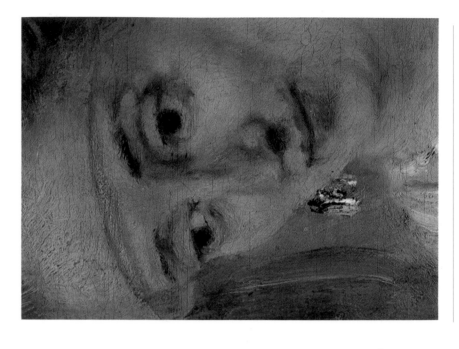

Fig. 35
Detail from 'Jacob Blessing the Children of Joseph'

SEE PLATE 35

The subject of this picture is taken from the Book of Genesis, Chapter XLVIII. The figures represented are the dying patriarch, Jacob, his son Joseph, and Joseph's wife and two sons, Menasseh (left) and Ephraim. The essence of the story as told in the Bible is the unexpected action of Jacob in giving the chief blessing (with his right hand) to the younger son, Ephraim, and the lesser blessing (with his left hand) to the elder, Menasseh. Joseph protests at this and tries to guide Jacob's right hand to Menasseh's head; however, Jacob refuses to change his mind and predicts that the younger son will be the greater of the two.

Most other painters represented this scene by showing Jacob with his arms crossed and Joseph reaching out and seizing one of them to correct the supposed mistake. Rembrandt's approach, however, is more discreet. He places Joseph close beside his father, with his right arm round the old man's shoulders, supporting him in the bed. With the fingers of his other hand, he gently attempts to move Jacob's right hand towards the older, dark-haired boy. At the same time, two fingers of Jacob's *left* hand – these are not easy to see – are placed against Menasseh's head, though whether to give him the lesser blessing or to move him aside is impossible to say. Rembrandt thus avoids the tussle associated with the crossed hands and Joseph's displeasure, and concentrates instead on the blessing of Ephraim. According to later tradition, Ephraim symbolized the coming of the Christian faith, whereas Menasseh stood for the Jews, and it cannot be by chance that Rembrandt gives Menasseh dark hair, while Ephraim is fair-haired and kneels

with his head bowed and hands submissively crossed over his chest, almost in the attitude of the Virgin at the Annunciation. The presence of Joseph's wife, Asenath (detail, Fig. 35), shows, however, that Rembrandt drew on Jewish legend as well as on the Book of Genesis (this was first pointed out by W. Stechow in the *Gazette des Beaux-Arts*, XXIII, 1943). Asenath is barely mentioned in the Bible and she is not recorded as being present at this scene, but one Jewish version contradicts this and says that she was summoned by Joseph to persuade Jacob to give his blessing.

Almost certainly painted in the year that Rembrandt was declared bankrupt (1656), this is one of his largest and most awe-inspiring religious pictures: 'powerful alike in its suggestion of inner emotion and painterly richness' (Gerson, in his edition of Bredius, *Rembrandt: The Complete Paintings*, 1969, under No. 525). Rembrandt's conception of form here is monumental. Large areas of canvas are covered with broad strokes of comparatively thick paint, on top of which he applied glazes. The forms, such as Jacob's sleeve, Joseph's turban, Asenath's dress and the bed-cover, are massive without being over-solid. The composition is uncluttered and direct, yet subtle. The mood is neither tragic, nor tender, nor serene but what can only be called sublime. The figures loom up before us, frozen for ever in their allotted roles, like participants in a *tableau vivant*. By any ordinary standards, the picture is an inexplicable achievement, created as it was at the lowest point in the curve of the artist's material fortunes. Yet artistically it marked the high-point of his heroic style of the 1650s.

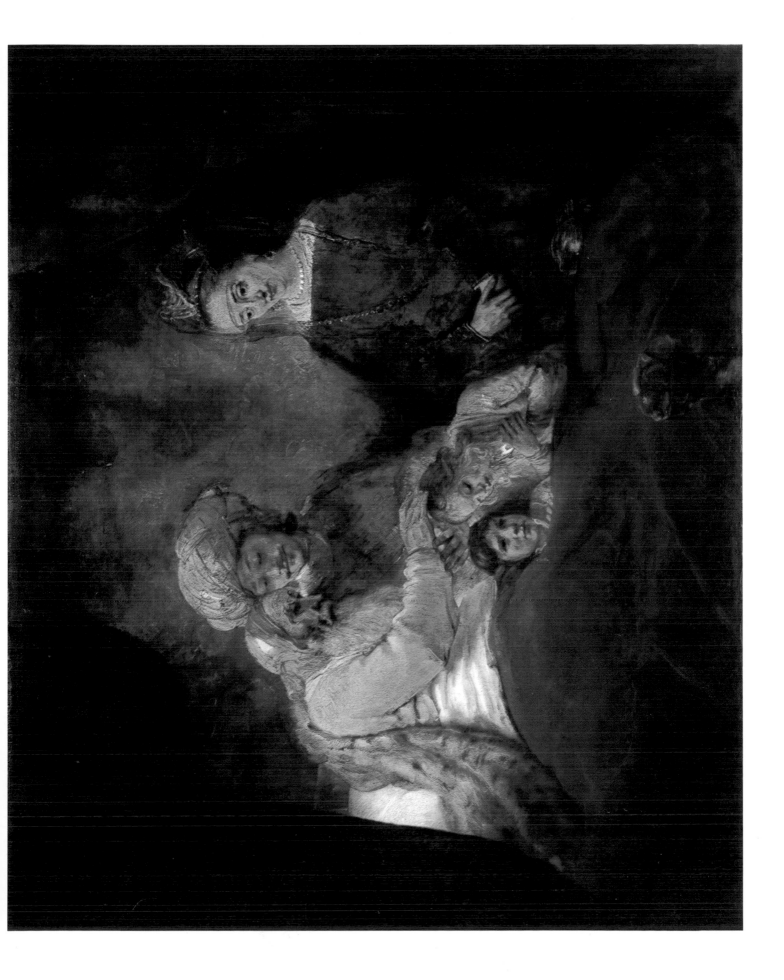

The Anatomy Lesson of Doctor Joan Deyman (fragment)

CANVAS, 100 × 134 CM. SIGNED 'REMBRANDT F. 1656'. AMSTERDAM, RIJKSMUSEUM

36

Like *The Anatomy Lesson of Doctor Tulp* (Plate 8), this painting formerly hung in the Guild-Room of the Amsterdam Surgeons' Hall; after belonging to an English private collector for part of the nineteenth century, it was bought by the City of Amsterdam in 1882 and deposited in the Rijksmuseum in 1885.

A large part of the picture was destroyed by fire in 1723; it has been calculated that the original dimensions were about 210 × 270 cm. A drawing by Rembrandt in the Print Room of the Rijksmuseum (Ben. 1175) shows the layout of the composition. The corpse was centrally placed with the anatomist standing behind it, backed by what is apparently a large canopied throne. Four figures were grouped on each side, one of whom – the assistant holding the removed part of the skull – can be seen in the part of the picture which survives. The symmetry of the arrangement, the steeply foreshortened corpse and the static poses offer a striking contrast to *The Anatomy Lesson of Doctor Tulp* painted twenty-four years earlier.

The body is opened at the stomach, which presumably indicates that the picture represented a public, not a private, anatomy lesson, al-though to judge from the drawing the space was somewhat confined. The criminal was Joris Fonteyn, who was hanged for theft on 27 January 1656. The surgeon, Dr Joan Deyman (1620–66), succeeded Dr Nicolaes Tulp as chief anatomist and *praelector* of the Surgeons' Guild of Amsterdam in 1653. The painting was seen in 1781 by Sir Joshua Reynolds, who vividly described the rendering of the dead body, 'which is so much foreshortened that the hands and the feet almost touch each other: the dead man lies on his back with his feet towards the spectator. There is something sublime in the character of the head, which reminds one of Michael Angelo; the whole is finely painted, the colouring much like Titian.' The drawing mentioned above shows not only the composition but also the frame; in fact it has been plausibly argued that this drawing was made after the picture was finished, as a study for the frame. Pilasters are shown at either side, together with a base below and a carved, broken pediment above. It would have set the painting in a kind of tabernacle, of a type similar to the painted frame which surrounds *The Holy Family with a Cat* (Plate 23).

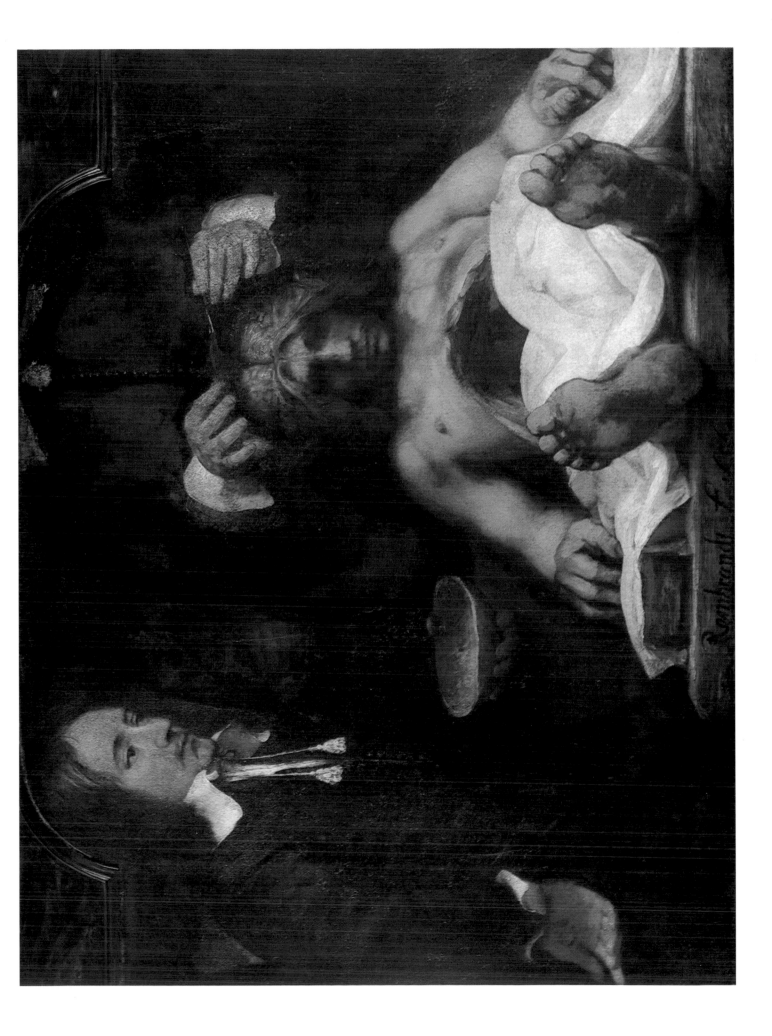

37

Jupiter and Mercury Visiting Philemon and Baucis

PANEL, 54.5 × 68.5 CM. SIGNED 'REMBRANDT F. 1658'. WASHINGTON D.C., NATIONAL GALLERY OF ART

This is a rare instance from the later part of Rembrandt's career of his using a subject from Ovid's *Metamorphoses*. Even so, the picture has more the atmosphere of a religious scene than an episode from classical mythology. The two gods do not wear antique drapery or show the usual partial nudity; the setting is the interior of a Dutch cottage; and a mystic light glows in one corner of the space, leaving much of the rest in shadow. In treatment, this picture might almost be a *Tobit and Anna* or *Supper at Emmaus*.

On the other hand, while it was typical of Rembrandt by this time to subordinate any subject to his artistic aims, his approach in this case was less eccentric than it might seem. Unlike most of the stories in the *Metamorphoses*, the episode of Jupiter and Mercury visiting Philemon and Baucis (Book VIII, 618–724) is entirely proper, not to say sentimental. It deals with such matters as marital fidelity, hospitality, trust and divine compassion and has, indeed, parallels in both the Old and New Testaments. The two gods, disguised as mortals, after being turned away at countless doors, are willingly given shelter by an old peasant couple, Philemon and Baucis. The couple provide the best meal they can and are about to kill their most precious possession, a goose, when Jupiter and Mercury reveal themselves. The gods invite them to climb a mountainside and, when they look back, they see all the country flooded except their cottage, which has been transformed into a magnificent temple. As a reward for their spontaneous generosity, Philemon and Baucis are made guardians of this temple for the rest of their lives. Distinctive in feeling as Rembrandt's picture is, however, it was not without precedent, for he was certainly influenced by an engraving after a painting of the same subject by Elsheimer, now in Dresden. Though Elsheimer did not go so far in eliminating the god-like attributes of Jupiter and Mercury and though he missed the emotional power of Rembrandt's interpretation, he had already found a satisfactory solution to the problem of the composition.

The painting here illustrated is one of the most charming of all Rembrandt's subject pictures, the figure of the youthful Mercury being particularly appealing. The colouring throughout, though subdued, is beautiful. The drawing is simple and economical, with the lines being used not to follow the contours of the form but rather to indicate its position in space. The fine, straight brushstrokes lie either outside or inside the contour line, seldom precisely on it. The same techique can be seen in the pen-and-wash drawing of *Christ Healing Peter's Mother-in-Law* (Fig. 36) of about the same date. The style is less dramatic than that of the artist's earlier drawings but it expresses both movement and emotions no less vividly.

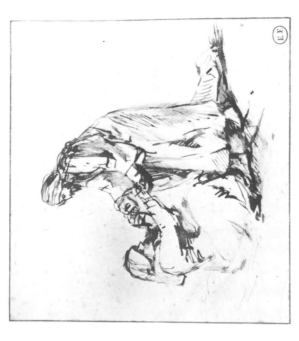

Fig. 36
Christ Healing Peter's Mother-in-Law

PEN AND BROWN WASH, 17.2 × 18.8 CM. 1655–60. PARIS, INSTITUT NÉERLANDAIS (FONDATION CUSTODIA)

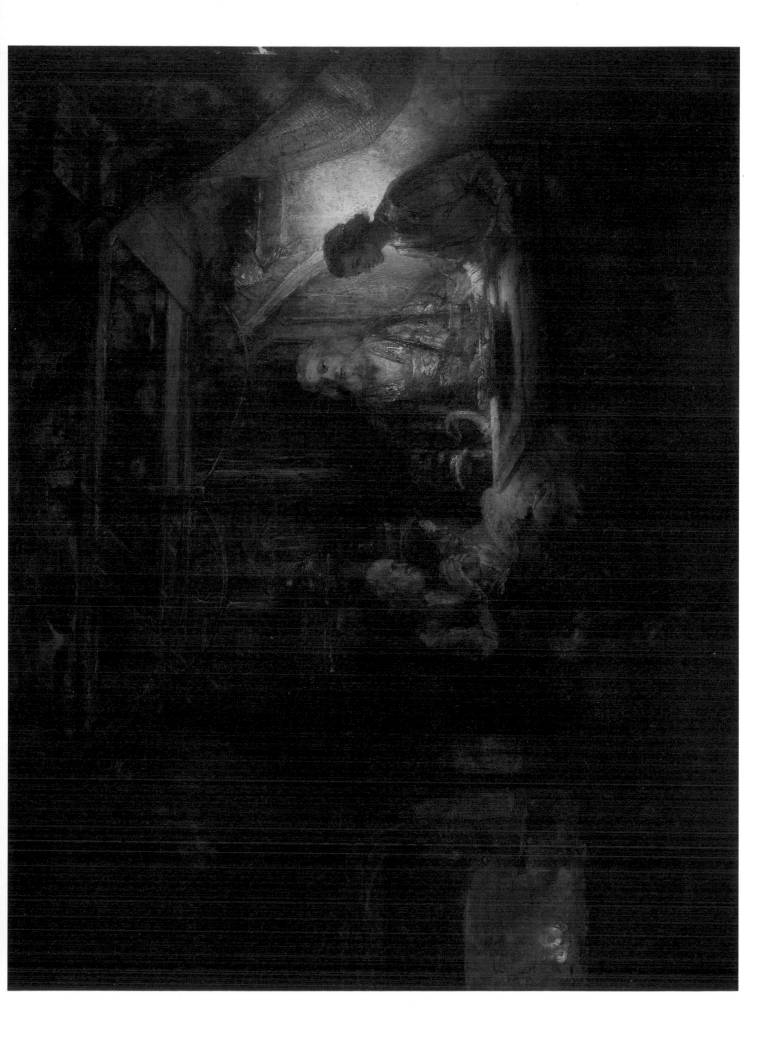

38

The Conspiracy of Julius Civilis (fragment)

CANVAS, 196 × 309 CM. 1661–2. STOCKHOLM, NATIONALMUSEUM

The subject is taken from Tacitus, *Histories*, Book IV, lines 13–16, which tells of the revolt of the Batavians, the original inhabitants of The Netherlands, against the Romans who were in occupation. The leader of the revolt was Julius Civilis (also called Claudius Civilis), who assembled the chiefs of the Batavians in a sacred wood under the pretence of holding a banquet. There he made them swear an oath to fight for their liberty. He is described by Tacitus as having only one eye, a fact which Rembrandt reproduces in the painting. The revolt was plainly seen by Rembrandt's contemporaries as a prototype of William of Orange's war of independence against the Spaniards in the sixteenth century and was a subject often treated by seventeenth-century Dutch painters and engravers.

Rembrandt painted the picture, which illustrates the first episode in the story, as one of a series of eight canvases (by different artists) which were designed to fill the arched spaces in the Great Gallery of the new Amsterdam Town Hall. He received the commission in 1661 and his painting was in place the following year. However, it was removed almost immediately for alterations, presumably at the request of the authorities, and it was never returned to the Town Hall. In 1663 it was replaced by a picture by Rembrandt's pupil, Jurigen Ovens. Although technical deficiencies have sometimes been suggested as the reason for the removal of Rembrandt's painting, the most likely explanation is the obvious one, namely that its style was unacceptable, both on its own account and because it did not harmonize with the styles of the other paintings (which were by the 'classicizing' artists, Jacob Jordaens and Rembrandt's former associate, Jan Lievens). It seems that Rembrandt himself cut the painting down and altered the central part in an effort to make it more saleable. In its original form the canvas was fully 5½

metres in both dimensions (larger than *The Night Watch*), with an oval top. A drawing in Munich (Ben. 1061) shows the composition before it was reduced. The figures round the table were flanked on either side by servants and onlookers, and the table itself and the conspirators were seen across a vast empty foreground, at the head of a broad flight of steps. Behind the figures was a backcloth and above that a huge vault.

Even – or perhaps especially – in its mutilated state, the painting is an incredible work. The handling is so wild and the forms are so primitive that it is not surprising that Rembrandt's contemporaries were repelled by it (assuming that they were). It would have been more than the seventeenth century could manage to see the style of this picture as the most appropriate imaginable to its archaic and barbarous subject. What is perhaps most remarkable of all is the colour, which is here inseparable from the lighting. As was so often his practice, Rembrandt places a source of light in the centre of the figure group, concealing it from direct view by the upper parts of the three figures in the foreground. Yet the amount of light emitted from this source is far greater than it would be if it were merely natural. At its most intense, the light is white; at a degree or two less than this it becomes pale yellow and suggests not just strong light but great heat. The image conjured up at the left of the picture is that the figures are not merely swearing an oath but are beating out their weapons at a forge, and even being hardened in the fire themselves. To the right and in the foreground, red is the dominant colour and this too evokes fire. In this picture, colour at last breaks free from *chiaroscuro* and becomes, for the first time since the very beginning of Rembrandt's career (when its character was very different), his principal means of expression.

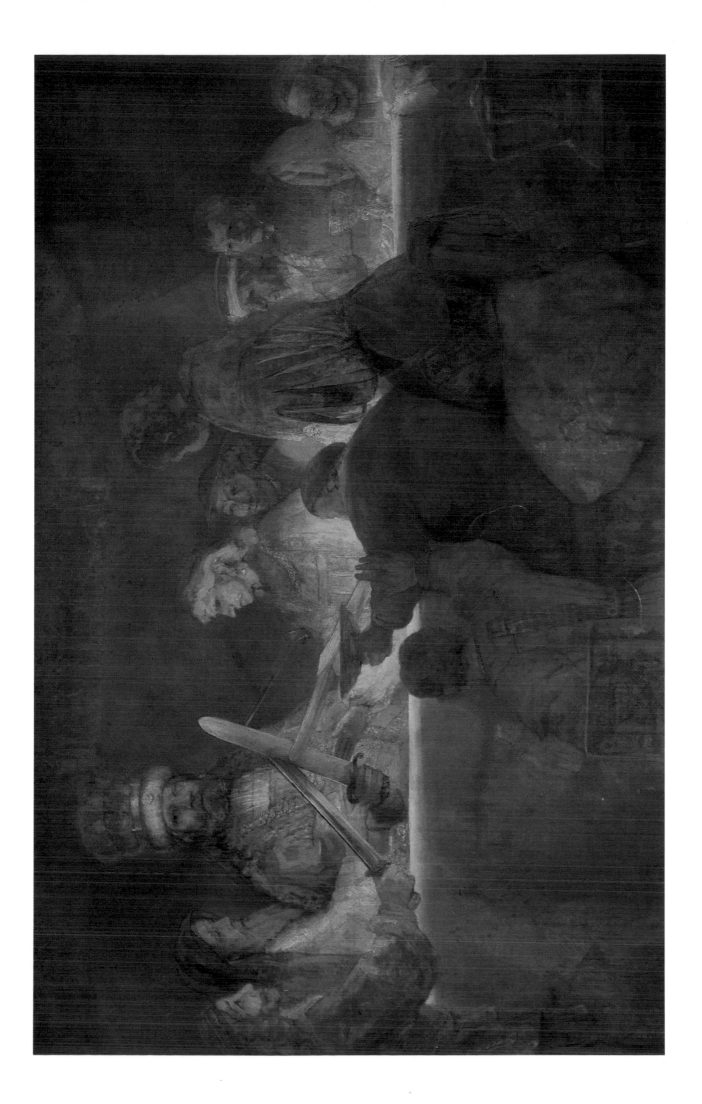

39

The Sampling-Officials of the Cloth-Makers' Guild ('The Staalmeesters')

CANVAS, 191 × 279 CM. SIGNED 'REMBRANDT F. 1662'. AMSTERDAM. RIJKSMUSEUM

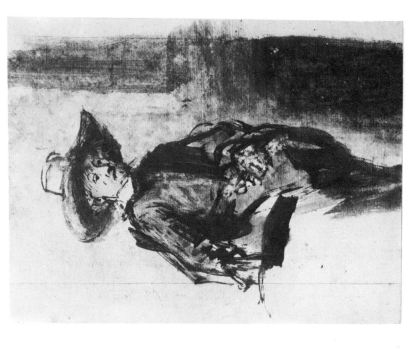

This painting, sometimes incorrectly called *The Syndics*, formerly hung in the Hall of the Cloth-Makers' Guild in the Staalstraat. It was acquired by the City of Amsterdam in 1771 and exhibited in the Town Hall, being transferred to the Rijksmuseum in 1808. The original signature and date, 1662, are on the tablecloth; those at the top right are a later addition.

The persons represented, whose names are known from contemporary documents, were the controllers of cloth-samples (except for the figure in the background, who is a servant). They were appointed for a year at a time by the burgomaster of Amsterdam to regulate the quality of cloth sold in the city, and the book in front of the chairman is probably the sample-book against which the cloth to be inspected was checked. They were not the governing body of the Guild nor did they administer funds, but were responsible directly to the burgomaster (see H. van de Waal in *Steps towards Rembrandt*, 1974). Thus they did not preside over a public meeting, and the popular notion that the figure second from the left is rising to answer an imaginary interrupter in the audience is a misconception. The main determinant of the composition is the pictorial requirements of the work of art, and Rembrandt considered the relationship of the figures to each other with great care. Three drawings (Ben. 1178–9 and Fig. 37) survive for the three figures

at the left showing that he tried out different positions for them, and X-rays of the picture reveal that the servant was also moved several times. As van de Waal has suggested, the low viewpoint was probably chosen not to indicate that the table is raised on a dais but to correspond to the destined position of the picture high up above a chimney-piece. Another striking, if not immediately obvious, fact is that the table is placed with its short side towards the front, not extended across the width of the composition as it appears to be at first glance.

However, if there was no imaginary audience implied by this picture, there was nevertheless a real one: the observer. At least four of the six figures are fully intent on him, and he is both the psychological and visual focus of the composition. The participants are as strongly concentrated on something outside the picture as those in *The Anatomy Lesson of Doctor Tulp* are on something within it.

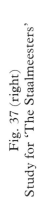

Fig. 37 (right)
Study for 'The Staalmeesters'

PEN AND BROWN WASH WITH WHITE HEIGHTENING, 22.5 × 17.5 CM. 1662. ROTTERDAM, MUSEUM BOYMANS-VAN BEUNINGEN

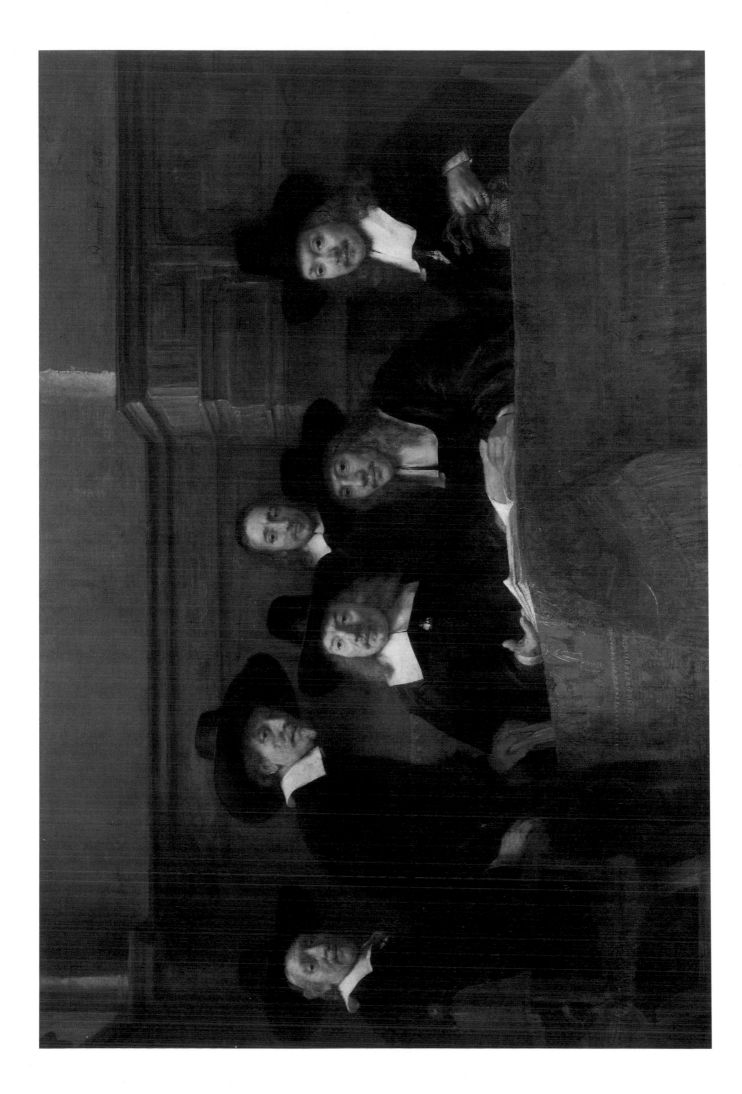

40

Portrait of Jacob Trip

CANVAS, 130.5 × 97 CM. SIGNED 'REMBR' (THE CANVAS HAS PROBABLY BEEN SLIGHTLY CUT). C.1661. LONDON, NATIONAL GALLERY

The means used by Rembrandt to express the sitter's character are discussed in the Introduction. Both the loose robe or gown and the cap worn by Trip are in fact unusual in the artist's late commissioned portraits, as, in such a context, is the loose and broken brushwork. Especially in the lower part of the figure, the folds and texture of the garment are hardly defined, and close inspection of the paint surface reveals a variety of muted colours which seem more to be those of the underpainting than the local colour of the robe itself. In view of this, it is possible that the picture was left not quite complete at the sitter's death. The companion portrait of Trip's wife, Margaretha de Geer (Fig. 38), is somewhat more finished in style, though it is equally impressive as a work of art and similarly austere in characterization. She wears a long black dress with fur trimmings and a ruff of a type which had been out of fashion for thirty years.

Assuming that the portraits were painted in the year of Jacob Trip's death, 1661 – and they cannot be much earlier than that on stylistic grounds – he would have been eighty-six at the time and his wife seventy-eight. She died aged eighty-nine in 1672. Both came from Dordrecht, where their families, and Jacob Trip himself after 1626, were leading iron-masters and armaments manufacturers. In 1660–2, two of their sons, who also dealt in armaments, had the palatial *Trippenhuis*, one of the finest Dutch town-houses of the period, built for them in Amsterdam.

The Trips were among the most frequently painted bourgeois couples of the period. Portraits of them by J.G. Cuyp, Aelbert Cuyp and Nicolaes Maes, as well as Rembrandt, are known. Another, bust-length portrait of Margaretha Trip by Rembrandt, dated 1661, is also in the National Gallery, London (Br. 395). These portraits must at least partly have been made for distribution to the sitters' numerous relatives, and it was on the evidence of a pair which had descended in the De Geer family that the sitters were first identified by Hofstede de Groot in *Oud Holland*, XLV, in 1928.

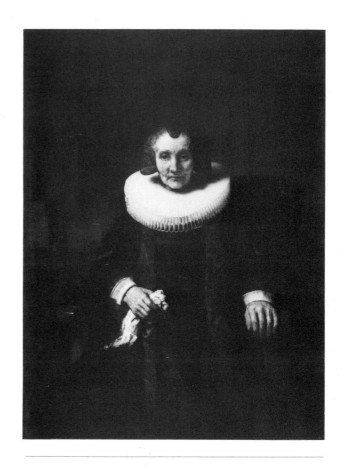

Fig. 38
Portrait of Margaretha de Geer, Wife of Jacob Trip

CANVAS, 130.5 × 97.5 CM. C.1661. LONDON, NATIONAL GALLERY

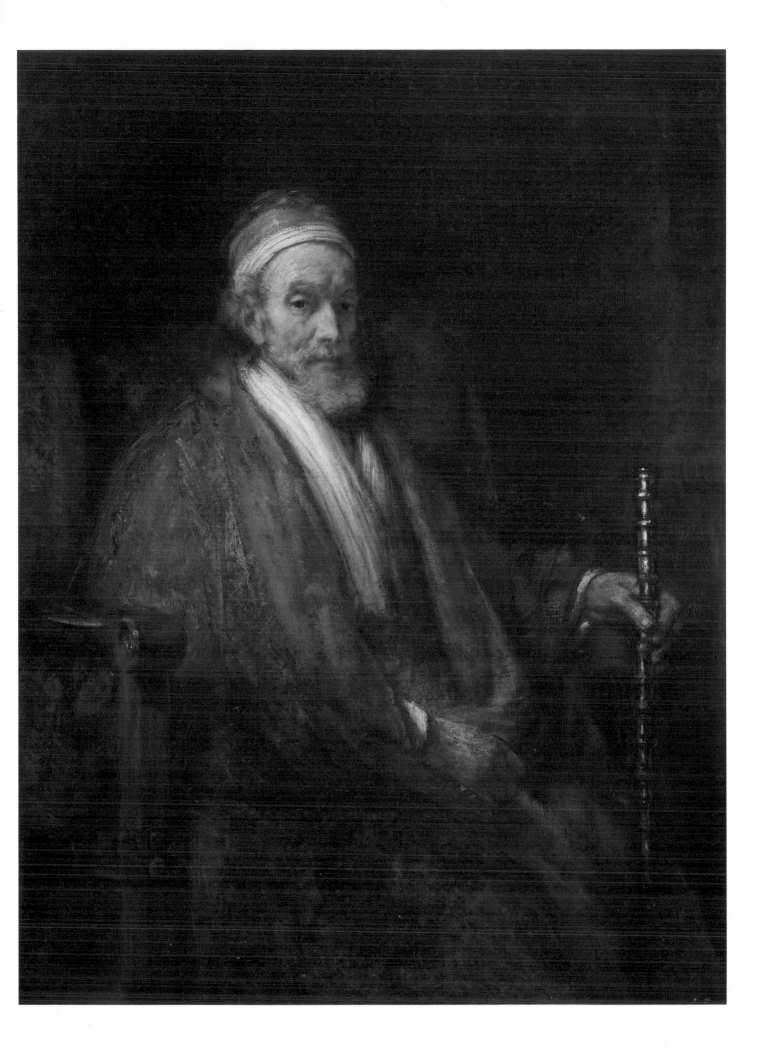

41

Self-Portrait with Palette and Brushes

CANVAS, 114 × 94 CM. C.1660–3. LONDON, KENWOOD, THE IVEAGH BEQUEST

This is one of the noblest and most poetic of all Rembrandt's self-portraits; of the three-quarter length ones it is also among the most personal. The head is fully worked up, the body much less so, while the hands are scarcely indicated at all. Being an 'unfinished' self-portrait, it would not have been signed or dated (though its authenticity is unquestionable). In conception, it still shows much of the breadth of form which the artist had favoured in the late 1650s, both in his subject pictures, like *Jacob Blessing the Children of Joseph* (Plate 35), and in other self-portraits. On the other hand, the forms have become flatter and the facial expression less aggressive. It is as if Rembrandt had wished to show himself as more forlorn. There is no play-acting here, as in some earlier self-portraits (see Plates 3 and 15). In the Kenwood picture, Rembrandt shows himself in the one role that was not a 'role' but the very justification of his existence: that of the painter who by his art is also a seer. He gazes out at the observer, defiant and immovable. This is an attitude which he seems to have made explicit in the only late self-portrait (detail, Fig. 39) in which his expression is not impassive. In that portrait, the smiling artist taps with his maulstick a statue of the Roman god, Terminus (a boundary mark), the implied significance of which is *concedo nulli* – 'I yield to no-one'.

The stylization of the forms in the Kenwood *Self-Portrait* springs from the aim of relating everything as closely as possible to the picture surface. Except in the head, there is very little modelling and no foreshortening. Rather than foreshorten the arms below the elbow, Rembrandt reduces one in length (so that it appears to be withered) and virtually leaves out the other altogether. Both the brushes and the maulstick are made to lie parallel to the picture plane, and the perspective of the palette is distorted to prevent it from receding into depth. The mysterious circles on the wall, though clearly behind the artist's head, reinforce the sense of a composition conceived as a surface design. No one has yet succeeded in expla ning these shapes satisfactorily. Some scholars have assigned them a naturalistic source, suggesting that they are the outlines of maps. Others have seen them in philosophical terms, describing them either as symbols of divine perfection or as emblems of the complementary principles of theory and practice (for which there is some justification in the emblem books of the period). Yet others have regarded them as purely abstract shapes intended to stress the geometrical framework of the composition. However, no explanation can be quite convincing which leaves out of account the similar circle (one, not two) which appears in the background of the smaller of two etchings of *The Writing Master, Lieven Willemsz. van Coppenol* (M. 80), of about the same date. In a later state of this etching, Rembrandt replaced the circle by a painting in triptych form hanging on the wall, which suggests that he did not regard the circle as essential either to the subject or to the composition. Perhaps the circles in the Kenwood *Self-Portrait* were merely provisional too, and he might have obliterated them or changed them into something else if he had decided to carry the painting further.

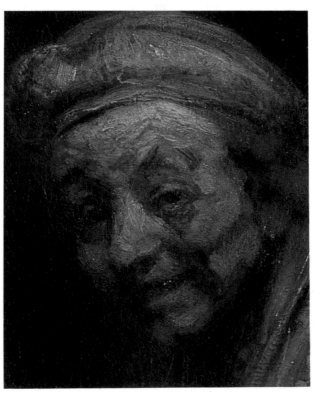

Fig. 39
Self-Portrait (detail)

CANVAS, 82 × 63 CM. C.1665. COLOGNE, WALLRAF-RICHARTZ
MUSEUM

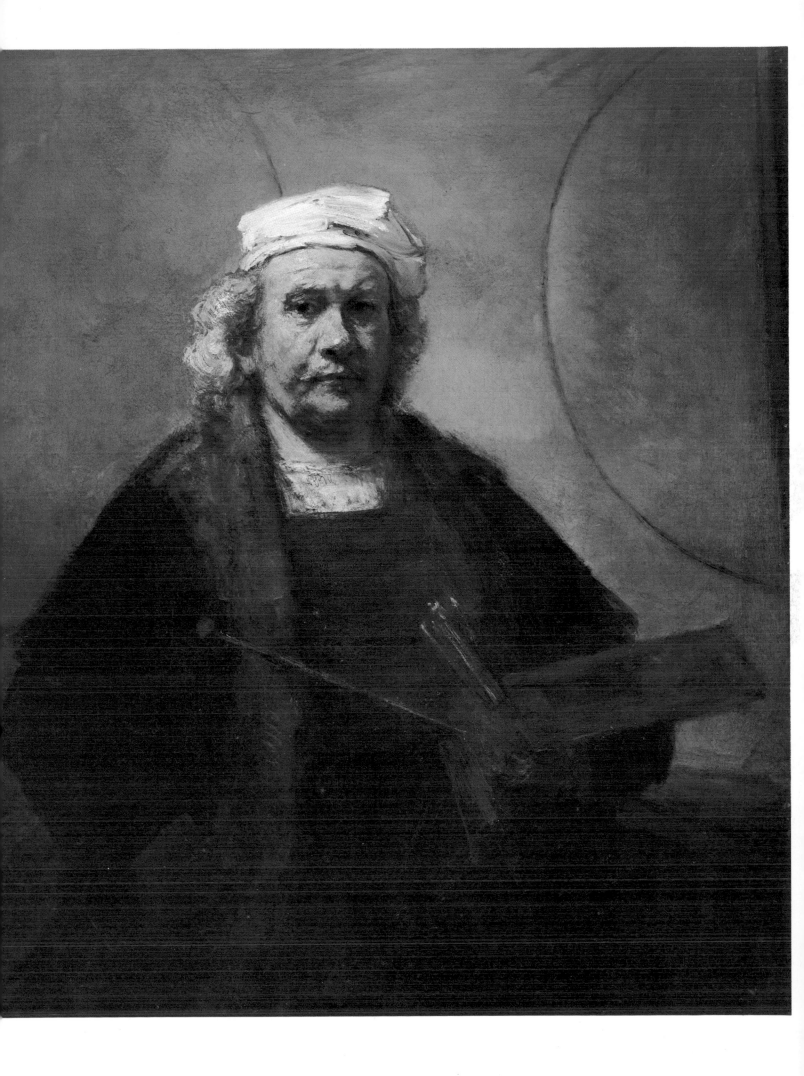

42

Self-Portrait as St Paul

CANVAS, 91 × 77 CM. SIGNED 'REMBRANDT F. 1661.' AMSTERDAM, RIJKSMUSEUM

The figure is identified as St Paul by the hilt of a sword (his traditional attribute) appearing in the opening of his coat. A book or, as here, a sheaf of papers, symbolizing the word of God, is also usually associated with St Paul. It was comparatively rare for artists to depict themselves as saints; it might be considered to smack of pride (though Dürer did not scruple to show himself as Christ). More often, in religious pictures, artists included themselves as by-standers or in some self-deprecating role, as Rembrandt did in *The Elevation of the Cross* (Br. 548), where he showed himself as one of the soldiers assisting at Christ's crucifixion. This is not to imply that Rembrandt glorifies himself in this *Self-Portrait as St Paul*. On the contrary, the mood of the picture is sombre in the extreme, and in this respect it is like the majority of the religious paintings and etchings of his late period. The beginning of this mood can be traced to the first version, dated 1653, of his great etching, *The Three Crosses*, in which the suffering of Christ, the drama of the Crucifixion and the mystery of Christ's sacrifice are the dominant themes. In the revised version of this etching (Fig. 40), produced by extensively re-working the plate about eight years later, the mood is even darker. Great curtains of shadow are drawn over large parts of the composition, almost obliterating the unrepentant thief and leaving space between them only for the dazzling heavenly light which falls on Christ. It is the climax of Christ's Passion which is represented here: 'And the sun was darkened, and the veil of the temple was rent in the midst. And when Jesus had cried with a loud voice, he said, Father into thy hands I commend my spirit: and having said thus, he gave up the ghost' (St Luke, Chapter XXIII, vv. 45–6). Rembrandt's use of *chiaroscuro* here is neither illusionistic, nor decorative nor merely poetic but expressive of the circumstances and meaning of the subject in the most literal way possible. An awareness of events as sublime and sombre as this, as well as his own misfortunes, is revealed in the features of his late self-portraits.

In the same years, about eight other paintings representing apostles and evangelists, using different models, were executed by Rembrandt – a new departure for him. They too are filled with a sense of foreboding.

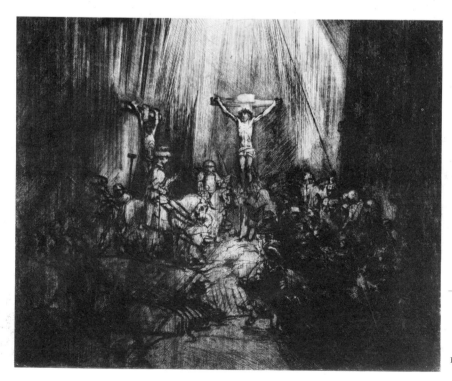

Fig. 40 (left)
The Three Crosses

ETCHING, 38.7 × 45 CM. C.1660–1. CAMBRIDGE, FITZWILLIAM MUSEUM

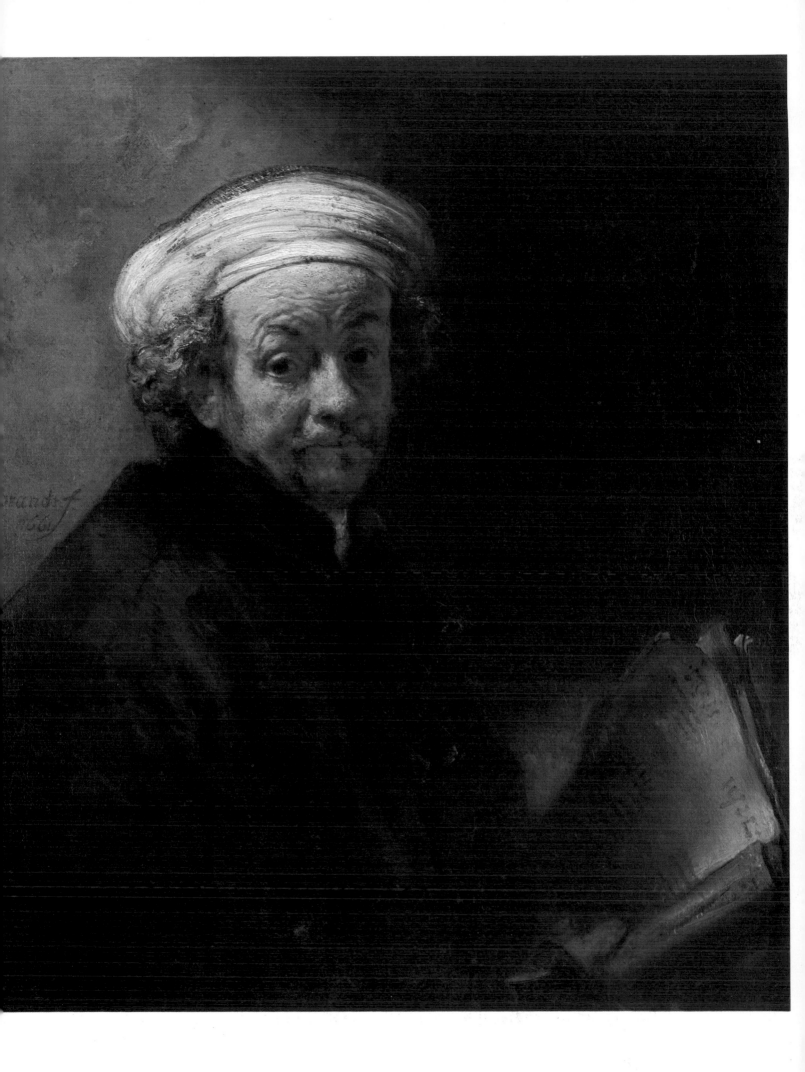

43

The Falconer

CANVAS, 98 × 79 CM. C.1660–3. GÖTEBORG, KONSTMUSEUM

In the powerfulness of its modelling and in its use of overlapping forms, this painting may be compared to the left part (with the man in armour) of *The Denial of St Peter* (Br. 594) in the Rijksmuseum, dated 1660. As in that picture, the placing of the figure in the front plane of the composition creates a dramatic effect which, together with the strong *chiaroscuro*, makes *The Falconer* one of the most vigorous and romantic of Rembrandt's late works.

In an article entitled 'Rembrandt's Conception of Historical Portraiture' (*Art Quarterly*, XI, 1948), W.R. Valentiner suggested that the figure was intended to represent the Dutch medieval hero, Count Floris V of Holland. This valiant nobleman was lured to his death by his former associates, Gerard van Velsen and Gysbrecht van Aemstel, on the promise of a hunting expedition. Despite being warned of the danger by a peasant woman, he trusted his companions, rode out to join the hunt, and was captured. This story was popular in The Netherlands in the seventeenth century and was often re-told, both in histories of Amsterdam and in plays performed on the stage. The suggestion that Rembrandt's painting represents Count Floris is quite plausible; hunting with the falcon was the Count's favourite recreation and he is shown in seventeenth-century engravings with a falcon on his wrist. In Rembrandt's painting he would be about to mount his horse, the melancholy expression in his eyes being due to the warning he had received. Whether Rembrandt portrayed an actor in costume or invented the costume, employing one of his usual models for the face, is difficult to say; on the whole, the latter is more likely, as the same model appears to be used during these years for other pictures, such as the Louvre *St Matthew* (Br. 614). Fig. 41 is an example of the type of oil sketch that Rembrandt may have made from this or a similar model.

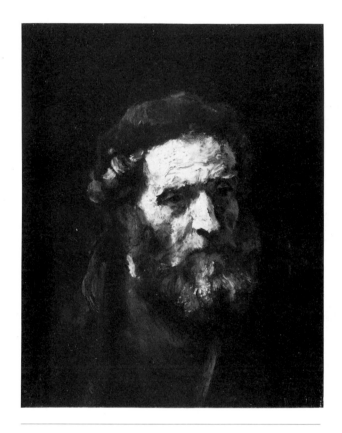

Fig. 41
Head of a Bearded Man

PANEL, 24.5 × 20 CM. C.1660. PRIVATE COLLECTION

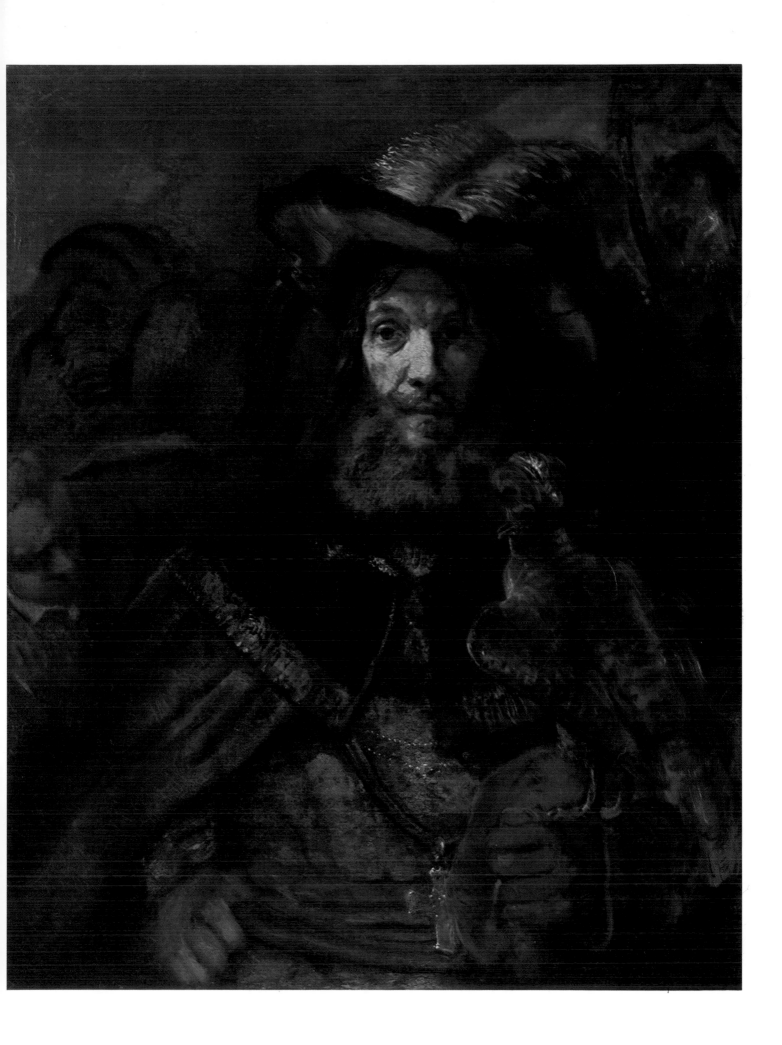

44

Two Negroes

CANVAS, 78 × 64.5 CM. 1661. THE HAGUE, MAURITSHUIS

Rembrandt's long-standing interest in the peoples and costumes of the Near East was extended in the 1650s to embrace the still more exotic regions of Asia and North Africa. His inventory of 1656 contained two items relevant to this: No. 203, 'One book containing curious drawings in miniature', and No. 344, 'Two Moors, in one picture, by Rembrandt'. The former has been thought to be the set of Indian Mogul miniatures which were later taken to Austria and incorporated in the decoration of the Schönbrunn Palace outside Vienna. Rembrandt made about thirty pen-and-wash copies of these miniatures (Fig. 42), and, while his exact purpose in doing this is unknown, the fact that they are so numerous suggests that he wanted the copies for reference rather than that he was simply practising. They show him responding to the awkward proportions, the lack of foreshortening and the facial types and costumes of Mogul art (though he could not resist substituting his own, more spirited pen-strokes for the hard outlines of the originals and adding some washes to indicate light and shade). What the miniatures may have suggested to him, or perhaps rather symbolized, were the advantages to be gained from abandoning the sophisticated, baroque means of rendering form with which he had been brought up and which he had been accustomed to use hitherto. Although the direct influence of these miniatures on his work was very slight, they represented to some extent a parallel approach to his own style in the 1660s.

Something of this can be seen in the angular shapes, flattened forms and seemingly casual composition of the *Two Negroes* (there are analogies here with the Kenwood *Self-Portrait* too). In fact it is unlikely that this painting is the one referred to in Rembrandt's inventory, although some scholars have claimed that it is, suggesting either that the date is false or that the picture was re-worked later. However, there is no real evidence that the painting was executed in two stages and, even if the present date, 1661, is spurious, it is likely to be right on stylistic grounds. Hitherto, negroes had appeared in European art almost exclusively in the scene of the *Adoration of the Kings*, one of the kings traditionally being black, but a few other portraits of negroes, including two oil sketches by Van Dyck, are known from the seventeenth century. Rembrandt's painting, however, is the most penetrating and realistic. At one bound, so to speak, he succeeded in rendering the entire negro physiognomy with perfect sympathy and fidelity.

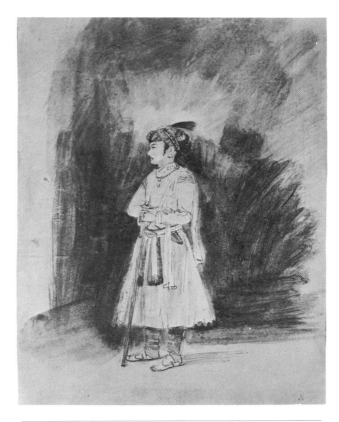

Fig. 42
An Indian Prince, after a Mogul Miniature

PEN AND BROWN WASH, ON JAPANESE PAPER, 22.5 × 17 CM. C.1656.
VIENNA, ALBERTINA

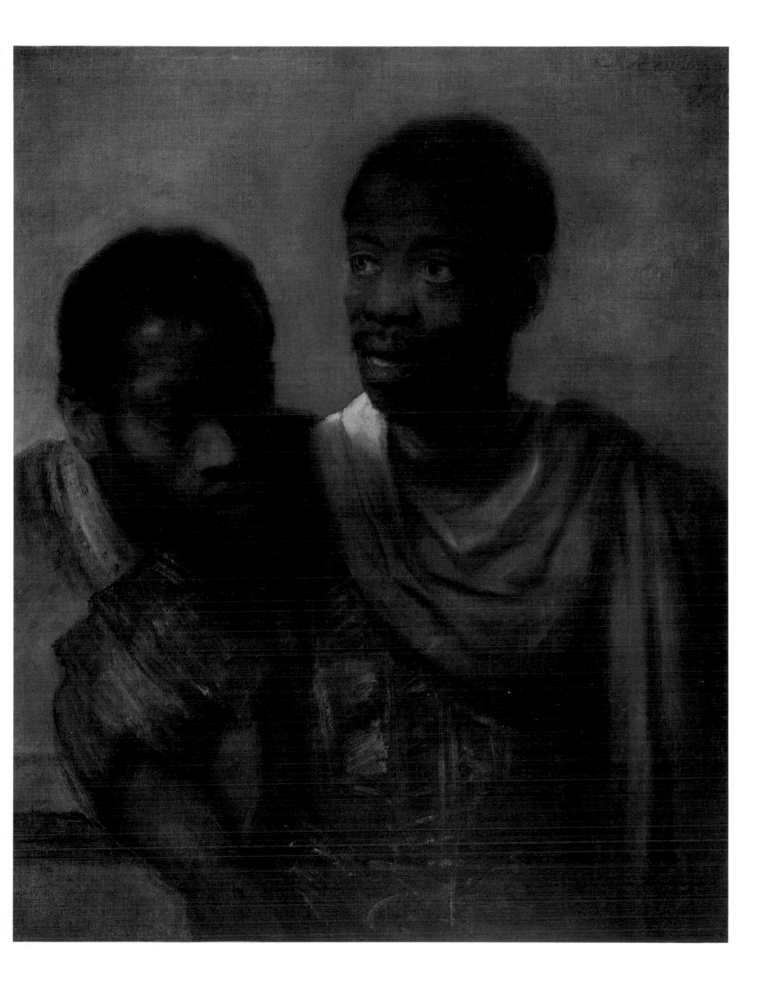

45

Portrait of Gérard de Lairesse

CANVAS, 112 × 87 CM. SIGNED 'REMBRANDT F. 1665'. NEW YORK, METROPOLITAN MUSEUM OF ART

The identity of the sitter was established early this century by comparison with the engraved portrait of him in Houbraken's *De Groote Schouburgh* (1718). Gérard de Lairesse (1640–1711) was a prolific painter, etcher and writer on art. Born and trained in Flanders, where he came into contact with the doctrines of French classicism, he settled in Amsterdam in his early twenties, not long before the date of Rembrandt's portrait of him. He became identified with the growing taste in the leading Dutch cities in the last third of the seventeenth century for French fashions in the theatre, literature and manners. His own painting was decorative and 'baroque-classical' in style, at the opposite extreme from Rembrandt's. Lairesse went blind in 1689–90 and from then on devoted himself to art theory. His major work, *Het Groot Schilderboek* (1707), was a comprehensive guide to current international artistic theory and practice and was translated into several languages, including English. It remained in- use in North European academies of art throughout the eighteenth century.

It would be intriguing to know what impression this young, cosmopolitan, literary and fashion-conscious painter made on the ageing Rembrandt during their sessions together – though it is a tribute to Rembrandt's international fame that Lairesse should have wanted to sit to an artist who was comparatively unpopular. Rembrandt portrays him with something of the vigour and elegance he used for the *Portrait of a Man Holding Gloves* (Fig. 44), but the treatment here is less formal as the sitter is a fellow artist. It is interesting to compare this portrait with van der Helst's *Portrait of the Painter, Paulus Potter* (Fig. 43) of eleven years earlier. The juxtaposition of the two shows that, once the *chiaroscuro* is penetrated, the designs of Rembrandt's late commissioned portraits are not so utterly different from those of more fashionable artists of the time as is often supposed. Rembrandt, too, created bold and well-balanced com-

positions, with sweeping, confidently articulated forms and an easy, decorative use of the blacks and whites, relieved by the colour of the sitter's hair, of contemporary costume. Where he differs is in achieving so much more than this: a sense of inner life and of the involvement of the individual in the fate of mankind.

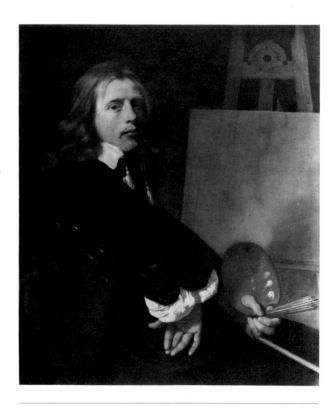

Fig. 43
BARTHOLOMAEUS VAN DER HELST
Portrait of the Painter, Paulus Potter

CANVAS, 90 × 80 CM. 1654. THE HAGUE, MAURITSHUIS

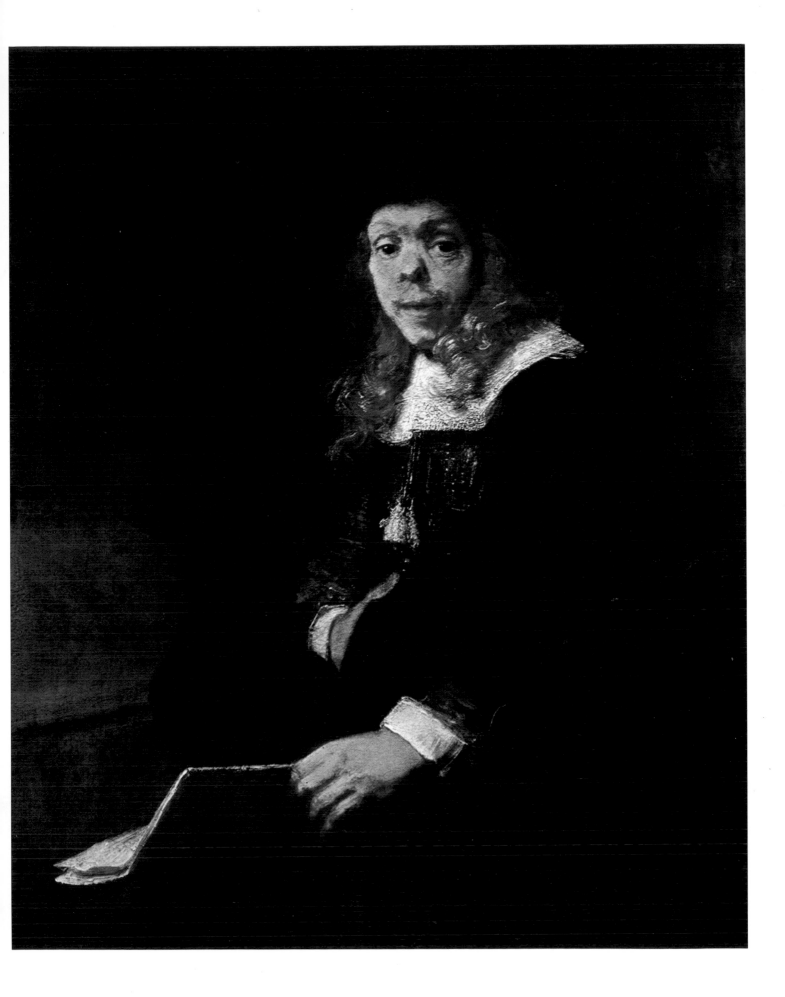

46

Portrait of a Woman Holding an Ostrich-Feather Fan

CANVAS, 99.5 × 83 CM. SIGNED 'REMBRANDT F. 166.' WASHINGTON D.C., NATIONAL GALLERY OF ART

This painting and the companion portrait of the sitter's husband (Fig. 44) seem to belong to the last two or three years of the artist's life. This is suggested by the very strong *chiaroscuro*, the abstractedness of the facial expressions and the quietness of the poses. On the other hand, it would be unwise to read too coherent a stylistic development into the work of Rembrandt's last decade. In common with most artists, his development slowed down in late middle-age, while his style varied more than before in response to the occasion. During the 1660s, for reasons which remain mysterious, the Amsterdam merchants and upper bourgeoisie returned to Rembrandt for their portraits in some numbers (though fewer than in the 1630s), and he would have considered it inappropriate to use too experimental a manner for such works. While never betraying the essence of his art, he adapted the surface qualities of his style as necessary and became as forceful a portrait painter in the current idiom as anyone. The *Man Holding Gloves* and the *Woman Holding an Ostrich-Feather Fan* are eloquent testimony to this.

It is not known who the sitters were and it may be suspected that Rembrandt did not know them very well either. He does not show the same insight into character as he had in the portraits of Jan Six or Jacob Trip (Plates 32 and 40). He concentrates rather on characteristics of rank and physical appearance and emphasizes the qualities of formal design. For the man, he uses a low viewpoint and elegantly turned pose, with the body in three-quarter view, the head looking more towards the observer and the hands held rather self-consciously in front of him. It is a type of pose that Van Dyck had made fashionable, and Rembrandt himself had employed it two or three times in the 1630s. The composition of the woman's portrait, though equally graceful, is more specific to its period. The pose is almost frontal, and Rembrandt makes calculated play with the shapes created by the two lighted areas. These form two equilateral triangles, the lower one inverted, with a band of black between them. The very dark backgrounds of both portraits, almost as dark as the black of the clothes, are further striking characteristics.

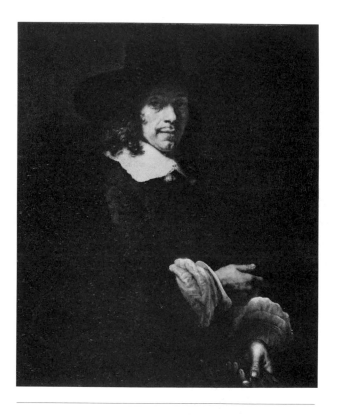

Fig. 44
Portrait of a Man Holding Gloves

CANVAS, 99.5 × 82.5 CM. C.1666–9. WASHINGTON D.C., NATIONAL GALLERY OF ART

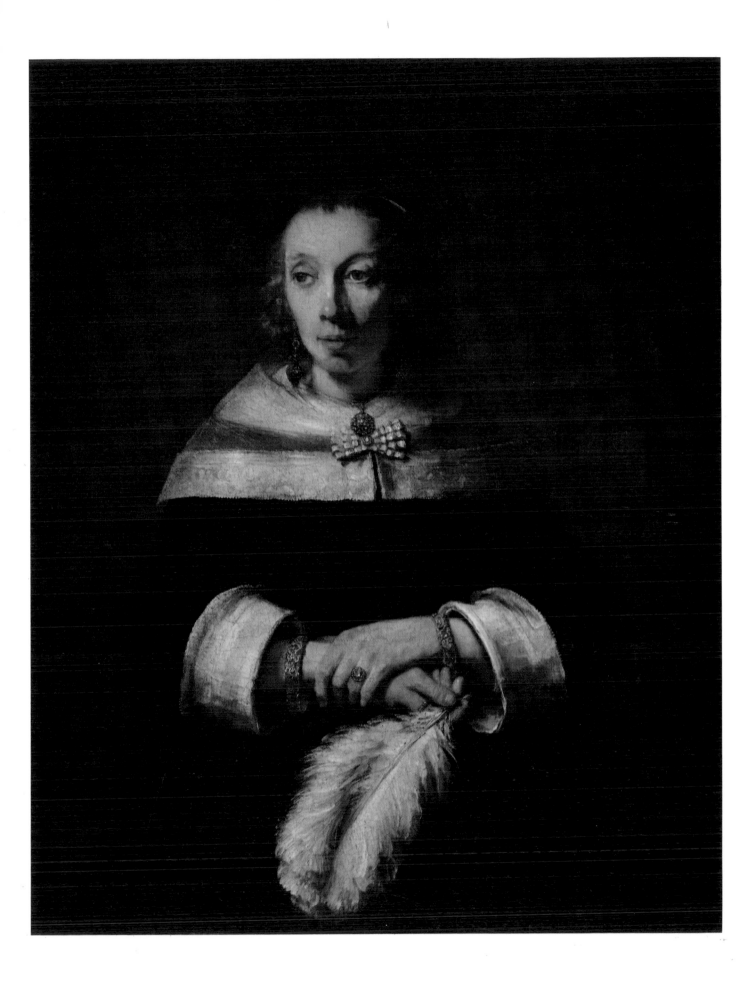

47

The Jewish Bride

CANVAS, 121.5 × 166.5 CM. SIGNED 'REMBRANDT F. 16..'. AMSTERDAM

Like *The Night Watch* and *The Polish Rider*, this is another misnamed or nicknamed masterpiece by Rembrandt which it would be insensitive to re-title. Nevertheless, the painting does not represent a Jewish bridal couple in the sense which the nineteenth century, which invented the present title, would have had in mind. The picture would then have been regarded as a romantic costume-piece, its very strangeness and aura of secretiveness suggesting that it showed some exotic rite, which was beyond the comprehension though not the sympathy of a predominantly Christian society. It is worth noting that the English connoisseur-dealer John Smith, who bought the picture in 1825 and also thought of it as a costume-piece or 'fancy-picture', called it *The Birthday Salutation* and did not connect it with Jewishness.

There can be no doubt, however, that an intimate relationship between the two figures was intended by the artist. The man places his hand on the woman's breast, while she moves instinctively to protect her modesty, in the classic pose of the *Venus pudica* which Rembrandt would have known from engravings or casts of classical statues. Yet the couple show every sign of tenderness towards each other, so this is not a common seduction scene (a frequent enough subject in Dutch painting). The theme most widely favoured by modern scholars is Isaac embracing his wife Rebecca while they were being spied on by Abimelech (Genesis, Chapter XXVI), which Rembrandt had previously represented in a drawing (Ben. 988). To summarize the Bible narrative, Isaac, staying in the land of the Philistines, passes off Rebecca as his sister, for fear that the Philistines might kill him in order to seduce her. One day, Abimelech, the Philistine King, observes the couple from a window making love in secret and guesses the truth, namely that they are man and wife. He reproves Isaac for the deception, pointing out that any man might have lain with Rebecca

'lightly', not realizing she was a married woman, and would thus have brought dishonour on himself and his people.

It is improbable that Rembrandt intended the full implications of all this to be understood by the observer of the painting, as he did in the case of New Testament subjects or his picture of 'Bathsheba (Fig. 31). Nevertheless, he would have known very well what the story was about and his choice of it is a further manifestation of his tendency to voyeurism (of which there is also explicit evidence in his last etchings). In the painting itself, however, he seems to thrust this aspect into the background, as it were. He omits the figure of Abimelech and concentrates on the love between Isaac and Rebecca. The pair could scarcely be more covered up and they embrace each other gravely and almost chastely. It is very possible that an actual man and wife or an engaged couple posed for the two figures, though whether or not the painting should be regarded as a portrait, with the sitters 'disguised' as Isaac and Rebecca, is hard to say. Some critics have supposed the models to be the artist's son, Titus, and Magdalena van Loo, who were married on 10 February 1668. Others, however, have described the man as middle-aged – which only goes to show how unspecific in these matters Rembrandt's late works often are.

All this apart, *The Jewish Bride* – to revert to its popular, unparticularized title – is one of Rembrandt's most poetic pictures. In mood it is intimate and serene. As a piece of painting it is almost miraculous. The forms are broad yet flattened, as so often in his late period. These forms provide a surface – or rather, a screen – on which countless overlapping brushstrokes of gold and red are laid, the colours increasing or dying away in intensity as they move into and out of the light.

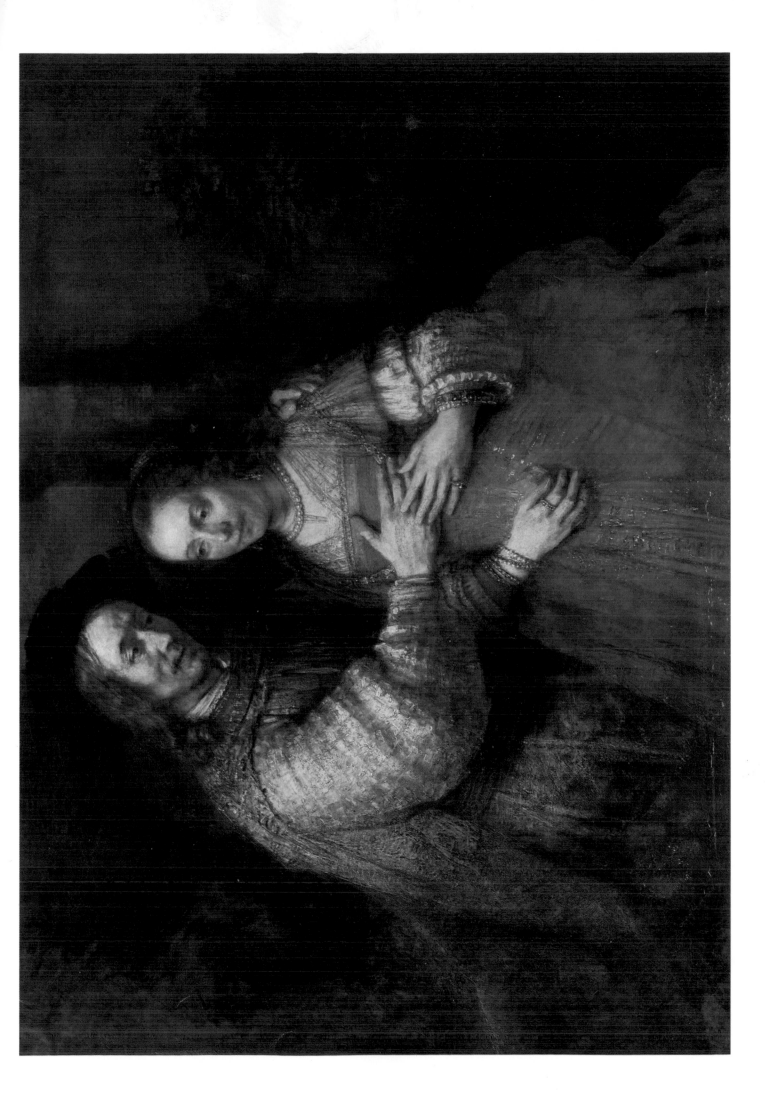

48

The Suicide of Lucretia

CANVAS, 111 × 95 CM. SIGNED 'REMBRANDT F. 1666'. THE MINNEAPOLIS INSTITUTE OF ARTS

The subject is taken from Book I of Livy's *History of Rome*. According to legend, Lucretia was ravished by Sextus Tarquinius, the son of Tarquinius Superbus, the last king of Rome, and after revealing her defilement to her husband she took her own life. Rembrandt had already painted another version of this subject two years earlier, which is now in Washington. In the Washington picture, Lucretia seems to gaze almost lovingly at the dagger as she holds it pointed towards her heart. In the later painting in Minneapolis she has already driven it into herself once, and her face has the pallor of approaching death. As Michael Hirst has observed (*Burlington Magazine*, CX, 1968, p. 221), the pose, set of the head and expression are startlingly reminiscent of Caravaggio's *David with the Head of Goliath* in the Borghese Gallery, Rome. It is not impossible that Rembrandt came across an engraving or copy of this painting after completing the Washington *Lucretia*, which prompted him to conceive the more brutal and pitiful interpretation illustrated here.

The motif of the hand clasping the tasselled rope, however, is a reminder of the common studio practice whereby a model posing with his or her arm raised (Fig. 45) would support it by means of a rope or sling. Rembrandt made a good many drawings of the female nude in his last years, often using this pose, and, although none of them is a study for this picture, the transition from the model supporting her arm to the dying Lucretia clutching at the rope would have been a quite natural one.

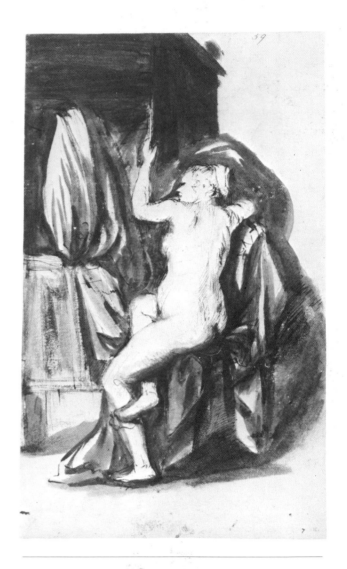

Fig. 45
Study of a Female Nude with a Curtain

PEN AND BROWN WASH, 29.8 × 19.3 CM. C.1660. LONDON, BRITISH MUSEUM

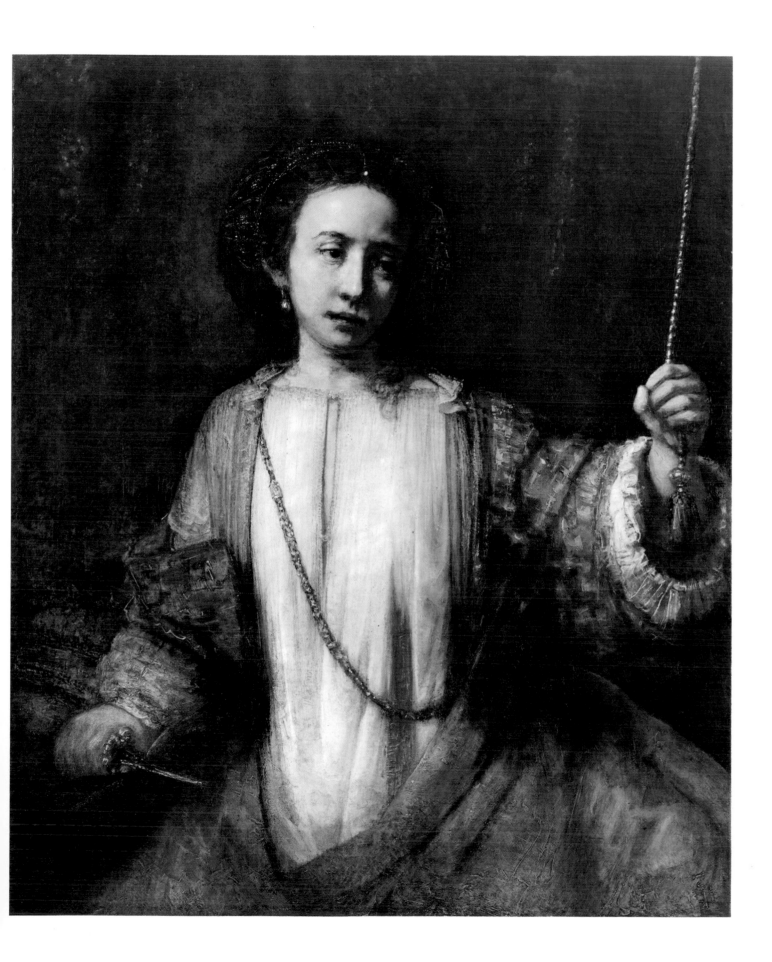

Select Bibliography

CATALOGUES OF REMBRANDT'S WORK

K. Bauch, *Rembrandt: Gemälde*, Berlin, 1966

O. Benesch, *The Drawings of Rembrandt*, 6 vols., London, 1954–7 (abbr: Ben.)

A. Bredius, *Rembrandt: The Complete Edition of the Paintings*, revised by H. Gerson, London, 1969 (abbr: Br.)

N. MacLaren, *National Gallery Catalogues: The Dutch School*, London, 1960

L. Münz, *Rembrandt's Etchings*, 2 vols., London, 1952 (abbr: M.)

C. White and K.G. Boon, *Rembrandt's Etchings*, 2 vols., Amsterdam, 1969

MONOGRAPHS AND VOLUMES OF ESSAYS

O. Benesch, *Rembrandt as a Draughtsman*, London, 1960

W. von Bode, *Great Masters of Dutch and Flemish Painting* (English edition), London, 1909

K. Clark, *Rembrandt and the Italian Renaissance*, London, 1966

J. A. Emmens, *Rembrandt en de Regels van de Kunst*, Utrecht, 1968.

H. Focillon and L. Goldscheider, *Rembrandt*, London, 1960 (contains the earliest biographies of the artist in English translation)

H. Gerson, *Seven Letters by Rembrandt*, The Hague, 1961

H. Gerson, *Rembrandt Paintings*, Amsterdam, 1968

B. Haak, *Rembrandt: His Life, His Work, His Time*, New York, 1969

J. Held, *Rembrandt's 'Aristotle' and Other Rembrandt Studies*, Princeton, 1969

C. Hofstede de Groot, *Die Urkunden über Rembrandt* (1575–1721), The Hague, 1906

J. Rosenberg, *Rembrandt: Life and Work*, 1948; 2nd ed., 1964, reprinted in 'Landmarks in Art History' series, Oxford, 1980

J. Rosenberg, S. Slive and E. H. ter Kuile, *Dutch Art and Architecture*, 1600–1800 (Pelican History of Art), revised ed., Harmondsworth, 1972

S. Slive, *Rembrandt and His Critics*, 1630–1730, The Hague, 1953

H. van de Waal, *Steps towards Rembrandt*, Amsterdam-London, 1974

C. White, *Rembrandt and His World*, London, 1964

C. White, *Rembrandt as an Etcher*, 2 vols., London, 1969

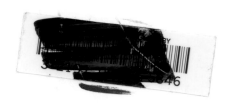